WITHL...

D1251265

Neo-Noir

The New Film Noir Style from Psycho to Collateral

Ronald Schwartz

THE SCARECROW PRESS, INC.
Lanham, Maryland • Toronto • Oxford
2005

SCARECROW PRESS, INC.

Published in the United States of America
by Scarecrow Press, Inc.
A wholly owned subsidiary of
The Rowman & Littlefield Publishing Group, Inc.
4501 Forbes Boulevard, Suite 200, Lanham, Maryland 20706
www.scarecrowpress.com

PO Box 317
Oxford
OX2 9RU, UK

Copyright © 2005 by Ronald Schwartz

All rights reserved. No part of this publication may be reproduced, stored in a
retrieval system, or transmitted in any form or by any means, electronic, mechanical,
photocopying, recording, or otherwise, without the prior permission of the publisher.

British Library Cataloguing in Publication Information Available

Library of Congress Cataloging-in-Publication Data

Schwartz, Ronald.
  Neo-noir : the new film noir style from Psycho to Collateral / Ronald Schwartz.
  p. cm.
  Filmography: p.
  Includes bibliographical references and index.
  ISBN 0-8108-5676-X (pbk. : alk. paper)
  1. Film noir—United States—History and criticism. I. Title.

PN1995.9.F54S387 2005
791.43'6556—dc22

2005007671

⊗™ The paper used in this publication meets the minimum requirements of
American National Standard for Information Sciences—Permanence of Paper for
Printed Library Materials, ANSI/NISO Z39.48-1992.
Manufactured in the United States of America.

For my wonderful wife, Amelia,
who likes to sit with me in the dark . . .

St. Louis Community College
at Meramec
LIBRARY

~

Contents

~

Acknowledgments

I would like to thank film director and critic Paul Schrader for his personal and critical comments, which fomented the genesis of this book about the style we now call "neo-noir." For Schrader, who was instrumental in defining the style of noir in black and white through 1958, there is only the "film noir trend." But many film critics post-Schrader, including Todd Erickson, Woody Haut, Foster Hirsch, Alain Silver, and myself, utilize a new term, "neo-noir," which is analogous to the terms "film après noir," "nouveau noir," "new noir," and "noir soleil." Some of Schrader's own films belong, ultimately, to this new "critical" category of style.

I would also like to thank the Department of Media at the New School for Social Research for giving me the opportunity to teach the first neo-noir film course in the nation in the early 1990s. One of the New School's most successful courses, it attracted such brilliant students as Ray Meola and Donna Lee. I must also thank Jeff Leibowitz and the members of the Romance Language Department at the City University of New York (CUNY), Kingsborough—namely Alfonso Garcia-Osuna, Gloria Pollack, and Franz Leconte—for their continual dialogues with me and other members of the Media Department. I would especially like to thank Dave Frankel for his encouragement of my teaching "noir" courses. Thanks also go to my editor Stephen Ryan at Scarecrow for his invaluable suggestions in the composition of this book.

I must also acknowledge Alain Silver for his book *Film Noir*, 3rd edition, which corroborated my earlier research with a section of its own appropriately titled "Neo-noir." A final thank you goes to Todd Erickson, whose 1988

5

master's thesis, entitled "Evidence of the Film Noir in Contemporary American Cinema," provides much direction in the undertaking of this book.

Also, I must acknowledge with grateful appreciation Howard Mandelbaum at Photofest, in Manhattan; my wife, Amelia, and son, Jonathan Fletcher, whose constant love and support helped me to realize the completion of this project; and Martin Scorsese, film director and critic, whose four-hour videotape, *A Personal Journey through American Cinema*, served to corroborate and inspire my own notions of noir and neo-noir. Also, I owe thanks to Jerry Carlson, producer of CUNY-TV, for his ongoing dialogues about noir and neo-noir; to Steve Feites at Evergreen Video in Manhattan, Matt Krim at Kino International Video in Manhattan, and Tom at Video Search in Miami, who came up with unexpected titles; and to my colleagues and fellow authors James Harvey, Andrew Sarris, and again, Paul Schrader for our continued dialogues; and to Bill Everson, a classy colleague at the New School who affected everyone's cinematic life here in Manhattan. Also, many thanks go to David, the manager, and Mr. Kim, the owner, of Kim's Videopolis at Columbia University for their continual dialogues with me regarding noir and neo-noir. Bless you all!

Also, my grateful appreciation goes to the English Department at Columbia University—especially Jonathan Haac, chair; Joy Hayton, executive secretary; and Dr. Ursula Heise—for permitting me to teach an innovative graduate/undergraduate course in the spring of 2003 based on my book *Noir, Now and Then*, published in July, 2001.

I must also thank my most perceptive students at Columbia University, where I was an adjunct professor of English and had the pleasure of working with Brendan Goetz, William Guyster, Rebecca Pollack, Gregor Staiger, Jennifer Stermer, and actress Julia Stiles. Their outstanding individual perceptions found their way into this book and helped make it a "pleasurable read" for myself, my colleagues at Columbia and City University, and all noir fans and readers.

I also have to thank Fran Mason, who wrote a paperback entitled *American Gangster Cinema: From Little Caesar to Pulp Fiction* (2002). His book showed me how to construct an alphabetical filmography for twenty-first-century perceptive readers, who are computer savvy and rely on the Internet for information retrieval, thus avoiding repetition of basic credit information for films under consideration.

One final personal note: because of the events here in New York City on September 11, 2001, my own personal and professional life have been irrevocably changed. However, most New Yorkers have gotten beyond this tragedy, and we are all back on track . . . hence, the authorship of this book since 9/11. We repair our bodies and souls, but we will never forget.

~

Introduction

Film noir and neo-noir are cinema styles that date to as early as the 1940s and continue into the twenty-first century. *Noir* is a French word meaning "black," and although "film noir" literally means "black film," it refers to the mood of the films made between 1940 and 1959 on black-and-white film stock, in which a male protagonist is usually led to his destruction by a femme fatale and winds up getting neither the money nor the dame.

The French critic Nino Frank coined the term "film noir" in 1946, and the French authors Raymond Borde and Etienne Chaumenton, in their seminal (and recently translated) critical work *Panorama du film noir américain*, used "noir" to describe a particular sort of cinema produced in the United States from just before and after World War II until the late 1950s.

Some American critics cite *The Maltese Falcon* (1941) as the first real "film noir," but I prefer to think of *Citizen Kane* and *Stranger on the Third Floor* (both 1940 productions) as the real start of American noir. Many pre-noir antecedents date back to the early 1930s, such as *Scarface*, and either *Odds against Tomorrow* or *Touch of Evil* (both 1958 productions) can be seen as noir's terminal signpost. It must be said that no American director during that period ever used the word "noir," nor did he or she set out to create a style or genre. It was the French critics who applied the term "noir" to this group of films that shared a similar photographic, artistic, and thematic style. Therefore, noir is not a genre, but an unconscious stylistic movement shared by many directors in 1940s and 1950s Hollywood.

It is also certain that societal influences contributed to the design of these popular films. Their thematic pessimism can be attributed to the post–World War II disillusionment of returning servicemen about a variety of issues, such as their replacement by women in the workforce and their lack of adjustment to postwar values. Coincidentally, there was a rise of acceptance of the new "hard-boiled" school of writers, whose escapist, masculine themes provided entertainment during the war years. The novels of James M. Cain, Raymond Chandler, David Goodis, Dashiell Hammett, and Cornell Woolrich were widely read and provided the "raw material" for films noirs. Also, because of new high-speed film stock and the ease of photographing outside of the studio (on location), real people and streets were used in a great number of films of the period. And finally, many émigré directors from France and Germany, who filmed in Hollywood and on locations, brought with them a style of "expressionist" cinema that developed in Europe in the early 1930s and reached fulfillment in the films noirs of the 1940s and 1950s.

There are many qualities and characteristics of film noir:

1. Chiaroscuro lighting (or low-key lighting)
2. Screenplays set in urban milieus filmed mostly at night
3. Frequent images of water and reflections of street life
4. Inverted frames (cameras held diagonally and/or vertically, reflecting the inner thoughts of the protagonist
5. Very complex and convoluted plots usually expressed in a voice-over by a central character, a detective, or a femme fatale who "flashes back" to the past

There is much violence and crime; eroticism and hetero- and homosexuality abound. Characters share obsessive behavior; males are generally untrusting and misogynistic, and become victims of their own paranoia. All of the aforementioned characteristics are framed in a pervasive darkness; photographers combine low-key lighting with deep-focus shots that provide a claustrophobic ambience. The viewer is constantly jarred by the editing of the film, always surprised by the asymmetrical compositions within the frame of the camera, the mystery of the plot, the xenophobia of the characters as they move through the darkness toward an unknown conclusion.

Neo-noir, the "new noir," is a direct outgrowth of the film noir style. Although most American film critics feel that either *Harper* (1966) or *Chinatown* (1974) is the first signpost for the emergence of the new noir, I feel it is Alfred Hitchcock's seminal film *Psycho* (1960) in which the reemergence of film noir begins, but with several new spins. Still a style and definitely *not* a genre, neo-noir has the following qualities:

1. Color and the latest projection technology (CinemaScope and the like)
2. A less restrictive rating system, allowing for greater screen violence, nudity, and harsher themes on screen
3. Remakes from the old "hard-boiled" school of detective fiction
4. Instead of good/bad detectives, screenplays deal with good/bad cops
5. The emergence of the serial killer

Where film noir always deals with con artists, petty gangsters, and psychopaths, these characters have been upgraded to grifters, techno-noir gangsters, and sci-fi psychopaths in a variety of new noir labelings that boggle the mind, such as "future noir," "agrarian noir," "techno-noir," "parody noir." But all these new noirs contain many of the elements of the 1940s and 1950s films, updating them from the 1960s onward.

My mission in this book is not to redefine film noir but to come up with a definition of the neo-noir style as a transposition of art, sometimes from original films noirs. I also hope to provide along the way some entertaining perceptions of the films under consideration and to show how these two unique styles of peculiarly American cinema reflect changes in American social mores.

So, neo-noir is a style of filmmaking that began in the early 1960s and fiercely continues into the present, showing the dark side of American life and dreams. This style includes crime, suspense, and thriller movies and has been created by writers, photographers, composers, directors, and actors who have insistently sought to encode and reinvent the darkest moods and motives of the American character.

Neo-noir, or the "new noir," is a film trend that is harsh and reflective of the cynicism of forty years of the Cold War, nuclear unrest, fiscal uncertainties, and the sexual revolution. Neo-noir tackles stories and themes not attempted by its stylistic predecessor, film noir: deeply corrupt cops, serial killers, psychopaths, and young fugitive couples running from the law, among other themes. Neo-noir contains doomed characters and presents melodramatic, psychological, detective, and western themes. It utilizes a vast variety of technical innovations that began in the mid-1950s with CinemaScope, VistaVision, and the use of wide screen and color. It also intensifies the violent aspects of earlier noir cinema and causes viewers to squirm, even flee the theaters.

The intense social climate in America of the 1960s and 1970s created a pregnant atmosphere for the emergence of neo-noir. A new generation began to question many traditional and prevalent values of American society. The highly unpopular Vietnam War was a great source of disillusionment. The Watergate scandal and the resultant impeachment of president Richard Nixon created an attitude of cynicism in the minds of most Americans. These events, among others, brought about a mood of hopelessness and resignation very much like the pessimism that reigned from 1941 to 1959, the peak period of film noir, neo-noir's immediate stylistic and thematic predecessor.

The neo-noir spirit boldly surfaces in entertainments such as *Psycho* (1960), *The Manchurian Candidate* (1962), *Chinatown* (1974), *Body Heat* (1981), and *Blood Simple* (1985). Among films of the 1990s, *The Usual Suspects* (1995), *Mulholland Falls* (1996), and *L. A. Confidential* (1997) carry forward an underlying spiritual pessimism regarding contemporary existence. The relationship of these films to the past is also crucial because the writers and directors make use of film noir models and moods, improving on them to help reinterpret and comment on the moral bankruptcy of contemporary America. A 1990s audience already had the sensibility to accept earlier film noir styles and ideologies, but the new films were in color and CinemaScope. We can assume today that viewers have a certain cultural advantage and have mastered film noir styles, so that they may read or decode modern noir or neo-noir films.

Like Spencer Selby's definitive work on film noir, this volume is divided into two sections: the first is an analysis of the thirty-two best neo-noir films beginning in 1960, elucidating the reasons why they indeed belong to this stylistic trend called "neo-noir." The second section consists of an alphabetical filmography and ratings of over 650 films made from the 1960s to the present. The filmography includes the film title, year of release, director, and a line or two about its essential plot and its pertinence to the neo-noir trend. Starred ratings after each title also enhance the reader's choices by indicating the very best neo-noirs, as well as some excellent, good, and even poor examples of the style.

When you write a "comprehensive" film book that steps into the murky territory of film style, and your intention is to guide readers through over forty years of American cinema and illuminate the cultural importance and broad appeal of this style of filmmaking, you always run into difficulties. The problem, particularly with neo-noir, is in selecting films that elucidate an in-depth approach and corroborate your views of those intriguingly dark aspects of the American psyche.

So, at the outset, let me state that the selection of films that this book encompasses is entirely personal. I have tried to acknowledge the "classics" as well as give brief nods to the popular films of the neo-noir style. Although Silver and Ward's classic book *Film Noir* (3rd edition) served me well as a basic outline, and Todd Erickson's master's thesis is the best in-depth work I have ever read on neo-noir, I have used them as springboards to enhance my own critical analysis of these styles. Fortunately, no author has a monopoly on film criticism, especially as concerns noir, après noir, faux noir, the new noir, and neo-noir.

As this book was going to press, there were so, so many articles recently written about neo-noir as a conscious genre (about which I still cannot agree). J. M. Roberts in an Internet article makes the case that neo-noir is greatly affected by color technology and changes in production code. He divides the "conscious genre" (his words) into eight categories. Two of his categories are remakes (the hard-boiled type) and faux noir, in which the conscious auteur/director deliberately makes a film that can be classified as noir, tech-noir, parody noir, pastiche noir, new age detective noir, con artist/small time gangster noir, or serial murder/psychopath noir (often overlapping with the film dominated by a good/bad/indifferent cop). These films, Roberts claims, are all style and no substance. Roberts's opinions deserve to be mentioned, though not necessarily adhered to. He also begins his appraisal with *Chinatown* in the 1970s and ends with *L. A. Confidential* in the late 1990s.

Also, in the summer of 1997, David Schwartz, film curator at the American Museum of the Moving Image curated a show entitled "Nouveau Noir," showing some thirty films made for theaters and television that represent the new noir style. Moreover, noir critic and writer Forster Hirsch devoted a whole volume to the concept of the new noir style, *Detours and Dead Ends: A Map of Neo-Noir*. His subtitle supports my contention that neo-noir is an accepted critical signifier and identifier of many crime films post-1960 that embrace the former film noir style.

One last note: neo-noir continues to permeate international cinema as well. The Mexican *Amores perros*, the French films *Crimson Rivers* and *With a Friend Like Harry*, the German *Run Lola, Run*, the Japanese *Audition*, and the Spanish *La mala educacion*, among many others, deserve a volume unto themselves.

So I offer my readers this book of fascinating ideas by a cinephile who has watched film noir as a child and has grown up and matured with the eruption of the new noir, or neo-noir. My feeling is that neo-noir as a cinematic style trend will continue beyond the millennium. For as long as there are men and women involved in crime and seduction, noirs will endure.

A Note about Ratings in This Book

Starred ratings for major films are as follows:

**** Outstanding
*** Excellent
** Good
* Poor
No stars: watchable but missable; for the die-hard noir
and neo-noir fan only

BEST OF THE
NEO-NOIR FILMS

1. PSYCHO**** (1960)
109 minutes, B&W

Director: Alfred Hitchcock.
Producer: Alfred Hitchcock.
Screenplay: Joseph Stefano, based on Robert Bloch's novel.
Photography: John L. Russell.
Music: Bernard Herrmann.
Editing: George Tomasini.
Stars: Anthony Perkins, Janet Leigh, Vera Miles, Martin Balsam, John Gavin.
Paramount. VHS & DVD: MCA/Universal.

Psycho is one of the most controversial films ever made because of its excessive use of violence and the power it exerts over its audience. Its excessive violence ranks it as the first new noir to have come out of Hollywood. It contains one of the most violent scenes ever filmed—the famous shower sequence. It is the granddaddy of all violence scenes because its shocks are not explicit. Rather, using Alfred Hitchcock's expert cutting techniques, set to Bernard Herrmann's incisive, slashing music score, the scene depends on what the audience "thought" it saw, not what it really saw up there on the wide screen.

Hitchcock's film was certainly a trendsetter for the neo-noir style. The film *Psycho*, although based on Robert Bloch's novel, was really inspired by the true crimes of a Wisconsin mass murderer named Ed Gein, who was arrested in 1957. Not only did Hitchcock introduce the theme of serial killing and all of its violence to the silver screen, but he was the inspiration behind some forty neo-noir films made from the 1960s to the present day. Also, neo-noir women are usually punished for transgressions or indulgences of questionable urges, as was Marion Crane (Janet Leigh at her sexiest) for her afternoon sexual encounter with Sam Loomis (John Gavin at his bare-chested sexiest) on a hot afternoon in Phoenix, Arizona. Hitchcock uses the violence of the shower scene as a punitive release for the plot's accumulated tension—very modern noir.

Some directors, like Brian De Palma, who may be the legitimate successor of Hitchcock, have capitalized on the latter's style and perhaps have based their entire careers on Hitchcock's genius. De Palma's 1981 film *Dressed to Kill* can be considered a total rip-off of Hitchcock's style of violence (e.g., its shower scene with Angie Dickinson) as well as of Hitchcock's use of tracking shots. De Palma follows Dickinson from one museum to another, a technique the director appropriated directly from Hitchcock's 1958 color noir thriller, *Vertigo*.

But *Psycho* is the original masterpiece, slowly paced, made with great detail, containing many scenes of sensuality and shocks, as well as many narrative twists and turns, as the master of suspense leads us to his controversial psychological conclusion. In 1960, *Variety* called *Psycho* "a shock melodrama with a couple of particularly lurid scenes [produced] according to the Hitchcock formula." *Psycho* was thought of as a horror film, filled with gore and two graphically depicted knife murders—deriving from Freudian motivations—with some interjection of humor so audiences would not take the film too seriously. The *New York Times* used expressions like "grisly shocks," "abundance of subtlety," and "old-fashioned melodramatics," but stated that, in the aggregate, *Psycho* "falls quite flat" in its denouement and as entertainment.

The plot of *Psycho* is intriguing. Marion Crane has a hot afternoon sexual liaison with her divorced lover, Sam Loomis, in Phoenix. Sam needs money to pay his alimony, and Marion returns to the real estate office where she works. A buyer leaves an envelope with her boss containing forty thousand dollars in cash, and Marion is told to take it to the bank. Instead, she pockets it and drives out of town with every intention of giving the cash to Loomis. As she drives on the highway, she decides to buy another car to avoid being traced by local police and is tracked by a suspicious motorcycle cop wearing silver-coated sunglasses. It begins to rain, and Marion is sidetracked to the Bates Motel. She meets the proprietor, Norman, whose mother lives in the gothic-styled main house high on a hill. Norman offers Marion a sandwich, they talk, and Marion goes to her room. She wraps the money up in a local newspaper and decides to take a shower. Unbeknownst to her, Norman sees her undressing through a peephole. While Marion is showering, the figure of a tall woman with long hair and holding a huge kitchen knife enters the bathroom and slashes Marion to death. Norman screams at his mother when he finds blood on her dress and the tell-tale knife (all offscreen), rigorously cleans the bathroom, and wraps Marion's body in a shower curtain. He takes her suitcase, the newspaper holding the cash, and her car and sinks all of it into the local swamp.

The rest of the film is a missing-person story—Vera Miles, playing Marion's sister Lila, hires a private detective named Arbogast (Martin Balsam) to investigate Marion's disappearance. Tracking the latter's movements, he ascends the staircase to see Norman's mother on his second visit to the motel; he too is killed by the knife-wielding mother. When Arbogast meets Marion's fate, Lila and Sam decide to investigate themselves. Lila goes into the fruit cellar after luring Norman outside on some pretext and believes she sees Mrs. Bates sitting in a wicker chair. When she turns the chair around, it is the skeleton of Mrs. Bates she is facing. Lila begins screaming and Norman, now dressed in a wig and Mrs. Bates's dress, tries to kill Lila. Fortunately, Sam Loomis overpowers Norman, who is last seen in a padded cell talking in his mother's voice. There is a pat psychological explanation given—Norman killed his own mother and her lover but could not live with the guilt of this crime. So he took over the personality of his mother through some kind of psychological transference and made her guilty of his murders. We do not know how many other cars and dead bodies are in the local swamp as a tow truck raises Marion Crane's car out of the mud. End title.

In retrospect, it is interesting to note Paramount Pictures was unwilling to produce *Psycho* until Hitchcock himself came up with the money through his own television production unit, Shamley. *Psycho* turned out to be one of the great financial successes for the film company and spawned no fewer than three sequels in the late 1980s, produced by Universal and all starring Anthony Perkins as a progressively older Norman Bates. Perkins's career zoomed, as he went from playing emotionally wrecked juveniles to effective serial-killer horror roles, clones of his original Norman Bates role.

In a 1998 television interview on the American Movie Channel, Janet Leigh called Mr. Hitchcock a "genius" and said she resented the insinuation that a body double had been used for the shower scene (Angie Dickinson had a body double in *Dressed to Kill*). Leigh even wrote a book about her experiences, entitled *Psycho: Behind the Scenes of the Classic Thriller* and published in 1995.

John Gavin worked mainly for Universal-International, often typecast as a handsome leading young man, and appeared in many films but had an undistinguished career. He later became ambassador to Mexico under Ronald Reagan's Republican administration. His costar, Patricia Hitchcock (who plays a secretary in Marion Crane's office), worked mainly in her father's films. Her best role was in *Strangers on a Train* (1951), in which she plays Ruth Roman's sister and is almost a victim of strangulation by the crazed homosexual Bruno Anthony (Robert Walker) in the elegant swap-murder plot. And Vera Miles's career never quite caught fire. Prior to *Psycho* she played Henry Fonda's wife in Hitchcock's *The Wrong Man*, in which she showed some depth as a distraught woman on the edge—possibly her best role.

But of all the work by truly talented craftsmen in *Psycho*, it was Bernard Herrmann's score that is best remembered. Herrmann wrote many neo-noir scores for many, many filmmakers up until his death in 1976, and his score for *Psycho* is one of the best ever produced for a Hitchcock film. The music behind those glorious titles (by artist Sam Bass), the famous shower scene violin slashings, and the music of the denouement are three of the most outstanding musical cues (compositions) ever written for American cinema. Herrmann wrote film scores in many genres—science fiction, sword-and-sandal spectacles, love stories, film noir, and neo-noir. In fact, he died one day after his famous score for *Taxi Driver*, directed by Martin Scorsese, was recorded for that film in 1976. Hitchcock's collaboration with Herrmann made *Psycho* a truly great film experience and probably the most influential film at the beginning of the neo-noir cycle.

Herrmann had collaborated with Hitchcock eight times. *Psycho* was their sixth film together; they had a falling out over what would have been their ninth collaboration, *Torn Curtain*. Herrmann's entire score was replaced by that of English composer John Addison, and Hitchcock never again worked with Herrmann after 1966. The rejected score has found its way onto CD and can be compared to the Addison one.

One other note of importance: Saul Bass designed the beginning and end titles, which segue so beautifully with Herrmann's masterful score. Bass also served as photographic consultant on the shower scene and designed the remarkable titles and dream sequence in Hitchcock's earlier color noir masterpiece *Vertigo*. Bass began his career in Hollywood as a designer. His talent was first recognized by director Otto Preminger, who hired Bass to do the titles in 1955 for *The Man with the Golden Arm*, still one of Bass's most original film title designs. But Alfred Hitchcock, with *Psycho*, was the galvanizing influence who extricated their best work from all of the talented professionals mentioned above. He created a new noir style that would influence the next forty years of American films and filmmakers.

Coincidentally, it was also in 1960 that English director Michael Powell made *Peeping Tom*, a color film about a serial-killing photographer in London, but without the Hitchcock shocks or black humor. The ultimate travesty is Gus Van Sant's remake of the original *Psycho* in color in 1998. Although the director follows the scenes accurately, there are no surprises in this film version, and all the actors—including Vince Vaughn in the Norman Bates role and Anne Heche in the Marion Crane role—come off badly, giving limited, tepid performances. The only real surprise is Robert Foster as the psychiatrist who explains Norman's guilt due to matricide and his mother's jealousy, which caused her to murder anyone in whom Norman was remotely interested. Although Simon Oakland handles the role capably in the 1960 version, Foster's interpretation of the role is far more incisive, in keeping with truthful revelations in neo-noir films. Although Hitchcock suggests Norman's masturbatory behavior in the original film, Van Sant makes this explicit as Norman looks at Marion through a peephole. The most glaring fault of the color version is in Anne Heche's portrayal of Marion during the shower scene. Heche is vulnerable, yes, but Janet Leigh's steely hardness and beauty are etched more brilliantly in her demise. Leigh's performance is aided by the music and that fabulous Saul Bass concentric photography, especially in shooting the irises of Janet Leigh's eyes—an original concept that defies repetition by any director trying to do a remake of *Psycho*.

The original, even with its flaws, still shocks us forty years after its debut. *Psycho* is the breakthrough Hitchcock movie beginning a new style of horror/ slasher, serial-killer films that reintroduced noir stylistics but conceived of them in a totally new and updated manner. Combined with the latest photographic, projection, and sound techniques and a less restrictive rating system, which allows for greater thematic freedom and truth, these post-1960 films contain greater amounts of violence, nudity, and harsher themes not tackled before by directors. *Psycho* is the commercial black-and-white film on the big screen that started it all, and with it, film noir reemerged—now the new noir, or neo-noir, with several new spins. Clearly, Hitchcock turned a new corner with *Psycho* in remaking the American crime film.

2. UNDERWORLD U.S.A.**** (1961)
99 minutes, B&W

Director: Samuel Fuller.
Producer: Samuel Fuller.
Screenplay: Samuel Fuller.
Photography: Hal Mohr.
Music: Harry Sukman.
Editing: Jerome Thoms.
Stars: Cliff Robertson, Dolores Dorn, Beatrice Kay, Paul Dubov.
Columbia. VHS: Columbia.

"Crime doesn't pay" as a theme permeates many of the neo-noir films of the 1960s. And revenge was a popular motif of that era as well. So Sam Fuller, who wrote and directed this black-and-white film, without the advantages of CinemaScope, keeps the screenplay and his vision of a gangster-revenge melodrama tightly under control on the big screen. Fuller, a crime reporter for the tabloids during the 1930s, is a dynamic storyteller and director, given to making B action pictures with much brutal violence and corrupt and amoral characters. Such is the background for this gritty story, which stunned audiences in 1961 and 1962 and boosted Fuller to "maverick" status.

Gangster films are a favorite of film noir directors, usually shot in a moody style, with low-key lighting, on rain-slicked streets in urban America—*Kiss of Death, The Street with No Name, Somewhere in the Night*, to name just a few. Films like these usually deal with the rise and fall of one or more villains. What distinguishes this neo-noir from its predecessors is the director's insistence on the goodness of his hero, as played by Cliff Robertson—a "decent" petty thief out for revenge on the four murderers of his father. Also, this particular new noir reflects the rise of the crime syndicate of the 1960s, operated by multiple crime kingpins, respectable middle-aged men fronted by charitable projects, milking the public through their sordid deeds.

The film is loaded with interesting details—Sandy (Beatrice Kay), for example, collects dolls because she cannot have any children of her own. Tolly (Cliff Robertson) sports a houndstooth sports jacket, one he made himself in the prison's rehabilitation program, but really prefers clothing with polka dots. Cuddles (played by Dolores Dorn) is beaten by Gus (Richard Rust) because she refuses to make a drug delivery for Gela (Paul Dubov). She is saved by Tolly and likes the way the latter kisses her. Tolly recognizes her past and "knows what's wrong with her"; she is sexually promiscuous. Cuddles agrees to testify against Smith (Alan Guener) after witnessing the latter kill a bar girl, and only then does Tolly agree to marry her—after he wipes out the entire syndicate. Tolly realizes Cuddles really loves him when she says in a voice-over, "I die inside when you kiss me."

The intricacies of the plot are multitudinous—all depending on Tolly's use and abuse of people to gain revenge on his father's killers. By manipulating Cuddles, he gets to meet Gela, forfeiting fifty thousand dollars for a key of heroin to get into the latter's employ. While the film campaigns against teenage dope addiction and prostitution, its real purpose is to show corruption—how police chiefs are paid off (five thousand dollars a week) to look the other way or have their relatives killed. The syndicate itself is called the "National Project," and its headquarters is a huge building with a penthouse and swimming pool, where weekly swim meets are held for disadvantaged children.

Tolly uses his early acquaintance with Driscoll (Larry Gates) to ask the latter to write phony surveillance reports so one mob boss will turn on the other. Gunther (Gerald Milton) is blamed for turning state's evidence against the rest of the mob leaders and is immolated in his wing-finned Cadillac by Gus. When Driscoll refuses to write another such report, Tolly types his own version on FBI stationery, this time implicating Gela. Earl Conners (Robert Emhardt) reads the accusations against Gela and has him murdered by Gus after Tolly beats Gus; Conners stands Gela up by the door as Gela awaits Gus's bullets. Tolly reveals to Driscoll he wants to get married and leave Conners. Gus shows up with orders from Conners for Tolly to kill an accountant named Menken, whose daughter Gus had previously run down by car as she was riding her bicycle. Tolly slugs Gus and dumps him in front of the local police station, with a note pinned to him asking the police to check Gus's gun against the bullets that killed Gela. Realizing he has no way out, Tolly faces off against Conners. They wind up fighting in the pool. Tolly drowns Conners and is shot down by one of the latter's henchmen. As Tolly dies in Sandy's arms and Cuddles weeps over his body, Cuddles promises to speak out against Smith, so that Tolly will not have died in vain. The camera closes in on Tolly's clenched fist—his final act of defiance against the mob.

The dense blacks and overlit whites of the photography capture the bleak reality of the slum scenes, streets, and alleyways of the past (when Tolly's father was killed), as well as the penthouse luxury and swimming pools of the present. The narration, however, depicting the love affair between Tolly and Cuddles, is curiously "gray" in tone—not quite film noir, but film gris, perhaps because Tolly seems ignorant of his destiny. His revenge cannot be deterred by Cuddles, who is no ordinary femme fatale. In fact, Cuddles, too, is not very bright—one of the facets of the new noir film.

Director Fuller's women have foibles, and Tolly and Cuddles, although apparently lovers, seem dysfunctional in their relationship. Nevertheless, there is a kind of sexiness each actor displays—Robertson with that scar over his right eye and Dorn with her slightly weather-beaten look and wet lips. And they speak with exactly the tone and in the idiom of the streetwise tough people of this era, which makes the film absorbing.

In 1961, *Variety* called *Underworld U.S.A.* a "slick gangster melodrama made to order for filmgoers who prefer screen fare explosive and uncomplicated. . . . It is crisp with the right-sounding gangster jargon and remains absorbing." The *New York Times* reviewed the film as the second half of a double feature (*Mad Dog Coll* starring John Chandler was at the top of the bill). According to the *Times*, *Underworld U.S.A.* "was another of [the] old-fashioned crime entries, adrift in blood [and] the girls . . . adroitly steal the show from the killers and their hunters. . . . While the outcome is always predictable, Mr. Robertson's hero is not especially likeable or even convincing . . . [although] Mr. Fuller's directing is nimble."

Sam Fuller is essentially a B-film director and has made many neo-noir films. His films excel in their portrayal of brutal violence, with protagonists who are both corrupt and amoral, two of the qualities of the new noir style. Fuller, who continues to make films in American and abroad, is best known for his crime films, such as *Shock Corridor* (1963), *The Naked Kiss* (1964), and *Street of No Return* (1989).

Cliff Robertson excels in making thriller films, like *Three Days of the Condor* (1975), although playing villains is not his forte. He was particularly good at playing a mentally retarded man in *Charly* (1975) and won an Oscar for his role.

Dolores Dorn is a stage actress who had a brief Hollywood career, and her costar, Beatrice Kay, a former singer of ballads, appeared in this single film for director Fuller. The *New York Times* said of Kay's "honest acting, [it] cuts through the picture as straight as a shark's fin." Nostalgia buffs may remember Kay singing with William Gaxton in a Technicolored Betty Grable musical for 20th Century Fox called *Diamond Horseshoe*, made in 1944 for post–World War II release the following year. Kay plays Gaxton's long-suffering hoofer girlfriend and finally gets her man only after Grable grabs singer Dick Haymes for her own. Kay's acting talents were better developed by Fuller in this film, made only sixteen years later. Her mother-son relationship in *Underworld U.S.A.* gives the film a new noir dimension and is rivaled only by James Cagney and Margaret Wycherly in Raoul Walsh's 1949 noir *White Heat*. Fuller's film contains many unusual pathological details that raise it above the conventional crime drama it was originally thought to be.

3. THE MANCHURIAN CANDIDATE**** (1962)
126 minutes, B&W

Director: John Frankenheimer.
Producers: John Frankenheimer, George Axelrod.
Screenplay: George Axelrod, from the novel by Richard Condon.
Photography: Lionel Lindon.
Music: David Amram.
Editing: Ferris Webster.
Stars: Frank Sinatra, Laurence Harvey, Angela Lansbury, Janet Leigh, James Gregory.
United Artists. VHS & DVD: MGM/UA.

Fear generated by the threat of the "Red Menace" has always been a popular theme for film noir directors. Richard Condon's peerless political novel of the late 1950s served John Frankenheimer's purpose in fashioning a neo-noir based on the Communist threat to American politics. *The Manchurian Candidate* is a work of enormous talent, energy, and imagination, with McCarthyist overtones. It is a film that could have been made only in a free America, showing the underbelly of the American political system.

Also dealing with the sensitive subject of political assassination, the film preceded the shocking Dallas murder of President Kennedy by two years. Because it deals with this subject, since 1964, *The Manchurian Candidate* has received infrequent show dates, despite its artistic—and, perhaps, prophetic—merits. Artistically speaking, it has Condon's terrific story transferred to the screen by comic playwright George Axelrod (*The Seven Year Itch*); wonderful performances by Frank Sinatra, Laurence Harvey, Janet Leigh, Angela Lansbury, James Gregory, and Henry Silva, among other players; a first-rate photographic style with location shooting in Washington DC, and New York City by Lionel Lindon; and a plaintive, expressive music score by David Amram that recalls the screen melodies of Aaron Copland.

Before the credits begin to roll, we find ourselves in Korea during the 1950s. A small platoon is abducted by a Russian helicopter and flown to the Pavlov Institute in Manchuria, where Sinatra, Harvey, James Edwards, and others are systematically brainwashed at a garden tea party somewhere in "New England." Raymond Shaw, played by Harvey, is asked to indiscriminately choose and strangle a fellow soldier and then shoot the "mascot" of the platoon, which he does on command. Totally brainwashed, Shaw and the surviving soldiers do not remember the explicit killings, but experience many bad dreams relating to the "garden party."

Everyone feels Shaw is the bravest, most honorable, most loyal man of all—he has saved the lives of the men in the platoon and is awarded the Medal of Honor when he returns to Washington. But something is wrong.

Sinatra plays Sgt. Bennett (Benny) Marco, an intelligence officer who wakes up nightly with bad dreams about the garden tea party, as does black officer Corporal Melvin (played by James Edwards). Of course Raymond Shaw is *not* the bravest, most honorable, most loyal of men—he has been trained by Chinese Communist agents to assassinate anyone who his agent-operator designates for removal. When Raymond is asked to play the card game solitaire and the queen of diamonds emerges, he becomes a lethal weapon for the Communists.

Sinatra plays Marco with restraint and class. He shows his sensitivity in scenes of "illness" when the film relentlessly flashes back to the indoctrination period, causing him to sweat and nearly break down. During one of these episodes aboard a train, he meets Rosie (Janet Leigh), a New York career woman who immediately falls in love with him. (On an April 1997 television interview show, *Intimate Biographies*, Leigh revealed that her marriage to Tony Curtis was falling apart at the time of shooting. Sinatra suggested that the director shoot her four scenes very quickly, before she suffered some sort of breakdown herself. Leigh's dialogues with Sinatra are memorable and convincing, a professional actress's rendering of love under her own duress that gave the film considerable dramatic weight.)

Harvey plays Raymond Shaw with the right amount of restraint, as a man who is completely unlovable and headed for destruction. Angela Lansbury, as Raymond's mother, has the best role ever in her long film career. Married to a McCarthy-like senator, John Iselin (James Gregory), she pushes her husband into a Democratic nomination for vice president and succeeds! Iselin denounces everyone against him as a card-carrying Commie but takes his orders from Raymond's mother. Lansbury cannot resist any political opportunity and arranges for her son to marry a former girlfriend (played by Leslie Parrish), the daughter of a politically powerful senator. Lansbury then seeks to use the senator to persuade the party of her husband's political worth as a candidate for vice president of the United States. When the senator declares he will oppose her scheme in any way he can, Lansbury comes out of the "closet" as Raymond's operator, playing the queen of diamonds. She orders Raymond to shoot the senator and his daughter (whom Raymond has married just a few hours earlier, eloping to Maryland). She also sets into motion the remaining plot—to kill the presidential nominee at the Democratic convention at Madison Square Garden and have her husband take over the presidency.

The Manchurian Candidate is senator Johnny Iselin, and Angela Lansbury is the Communist power behind her brainwashed son, who is the instrument to push the Communists into power over our democratic government. At the political rally in Madison Square Garden, Raymond, thinly disguised as a priest, sets out to kill the presidential candidate. Meanwhile, Benny has discovered Raymond's links to the queen of diamonds. As Benny runs to the room where Raymond has the candidate in his gun sights, Raymond turns the gun on Johnny Iselin and his own mother in a spectacular double murder. Benny reaches Raymond at last while the latter is tying his Congressional Medal of Honor around his neck; in a real act of bravery, Raymond points the gun barrel to his head and pulls the trigger, saving America from the Communist scourge. This is certainly a new noir twist: the real threat is from *within* America, not elsewhere.

The Manchurian Candidate is a brilliant political neo-noir with excellent offbeat performances, a first-rate suspense melodrama that has, perhaps, a weak, nihilistic ending. In the last scene, Benny reads to Rosie a book about Medal of Honor winners, commending their deeds—but the story that we have just watched will never be published. Raymond Shaw will go down in history as a suicidal maniac and nothing more. But we, the audience, know the real truth.

Only *Variety* understood the importance and drama of *The Manchurian Candidate*, predicting it would be "one of the year's top grossers—a 'rare' film that works in all departments—story, production and performances so well blended that the end effect is one of nearly complete satisfaction." *New York Times* critic Bosley Crowther felt the film would "scare some viewers to death, if they should believe it." Because the film is so "artfully contrived, the plot so interestingly started, the dialogue so racy and sharp," Crowther could not suspend his disbelief that it was possible for a man who was brainwashed to commit multiple murders and remain "dutifully submissive to his brain washer's spell two years later." In Crowther words, "it is too bad [the film] has so little to put across."

According to director/critic Paul Schrader in his *Notes on Film Noir*, Janet Leigh made the "last film noir"—*Touch of Evil* (1958), directed by Orson Welles. She also appeared in *Psycho* (1960) as the unforgettable Marion Crane and continued to act in new noir films such as *Harper* (1964). Her last Hollywood film was John Carpenter's *The Fog* (1980).

Having starred in mostly musical films since the early 1940s, Frank Sinatra found a new career in dramatic films in the early and late 1950s. He played Private Maggio in Fred Zinnemann's *From Here to Eternity* (1953) and appeared in some new noir films in the 1960s, such as *Tony Rome* (1967), *The Detective*, and *Lady in Cement* (both 1968).

John Frankenheimer, originally a television director for *CBS' Playhouse 90*, began his film career in the late 1950s. The release of *The Manchurian Candidate* was suppressed for over twenty years. When it did emerge, the film's stinging political intrigue and suspense won the director a new cadre of fans of the new noir. Frankenheimer directed other masterpieces of this ilk— in 1974, *The French Connection II* and in 1977, *Black Sunday*. His directorial efforts otherwise have been minimal. *The Manchurian Candidate* is the great film that has cemented his artistic career. It is an exciting, nightmarish film, highly charged, imaginative, and powerful. Everything in the film carries with it layers of subtext, hidden codes, double meanings. And the photography emphasizes its Chinese puzzle box structure. Richard Condon, the author of the original novel, was pleased by Frankenheimer's direction and Axelrod's script. But as Angela Lansbury remarked, "The poor thing [film], you know, went from failure to classic without ever passing through success. It would be nice for it to have some success." Even Frank Sinatra—who pulled out of distribution his own film *Suddenly* (1954), as well as *The Manchurian Candidate*, because of the shared theme of political assassination—was glad in the late 1980s to see the latter film released and find new audiences. (Sinatra heard Lee Harvey Oswald watched *Suddenly* before he killed John F. Kennedy in Dallas.)

The Manchurian Candidate now plays quite regularly on the American Movie Channel and is easily available on VHS and DVD from MGM/UA. New audiences are finding this film to be deserving of its place in the pantheon of remarkable new noir political thrillers.

There is an interesting coda to this summary. Tina Sinatra (Frank's daughter) held the rights to the original *Manchurian Candidate* when it was pulled off the screen by her father because of the assassination of John F. Kennedy, with whom Sinatra was great friends. In 2004, she became the executive producer of the film's first remake, also entitled *The Manchurian Candidate*, with a screenplay by George Axelrod and two additional writers, Daniel Pyne and Dean Georgaris. Filmed in color and CinemaScope and directed by Jonathan Demme, this new noir version received an R rating for excessive violence and prurient language. The updated plot has Ben Marco played by Denzel Washington, with Liev Schrieber as Raymond Shaw and Meryl Streep as his mother. The setting is immediately after the Persian Gulf War, when Ben Marco, troubled by dreams of brainwashing, discovers his best recruit, Raymond Shaw, is a candidate for the vice presidency of the United States.

Marco also discovers that Shaw is the pawn (complete with microchip implant) of the Manchurian Global Corporation, which has ambitions to take over the entire American political and economic scene. Raymond's mother has sold her soul to the encroaching corporation and become its operative. There is no Communist threat here—just big business!

Brainwashed Ben Marco becomes the designated assassin of the presidential candidate; he will act at the voice command of Raymond's mother. But Marco shoots Raymond Shaw and his mother, then tries to commit suicide. Instead, he is wounded by Rosie (in this version, a CIA operative), who also helps him to discover somewhere in the Persian Gulf how the chemical brainwashing and conspiracy linkage took place; and a mind-controlling electronic chip is finally excised from the body of Ben Marco.

Comparisons between the two versions, other than those concerning plot points, are irrelevant. What director Demme has succeeded in doing very well is to update Condon's original novel into another dimension of conspiracy, utilizing high-tech images, color, and media resources to enhance a black-and-white neo-noir Cold War thriller that emphasized a nationwide paranoia over the threat of Communism. In 2004, the paranoia of subverting the democratic political processes emanates in the era of Halliburton, Enron, California's phony electric crisis, and other acts of corporate terrorism that have caused lives and fortunes to be unfortunately lost. The updated *Manchurian Candidate* stands on its own as a scarier and more cynical film, very much a reflection of its own era.

4. THE NAKED KISS**** (1964)
93 Minutes, B&W

Director: Samuel Fuller.
Producer: Samuel Fuller.
Screenplay: Samuel Fuller.
Photography: Stanley Cortez.
Music: Paul Dunlap.
Editing: Jerome Thoms.
Stars: Constance Towers, Anthony Eisley, Michael Dante, Virginia Grey.
Allied Artists. VHS: Allied Artists, DVD: Criterion Collection.

Always known as a "maverick" director, Sam Fuller wrote the original screenplay for this bold crime film, crude at times, but thematically vital and expressive, for it deals with themes never touched on before during the 1950s. Representative of the new-noir era, this was the first film about pedophiles and their excessive aberrations. Even the title is explained by the protagonist, a former prostitute, as meaning the "kiss of a pervert."

The Naked Kiss opens with a spectacular scene—a woman is beating a man unconscious with her spiked-heel shoe to obtain money he stole from her. Apparently, that man was her pimp, and Kelly (played magnificently by Constance Towers) was a prostitute in his employ; he held out seventy-five dollars from her fee. During the beating, Kelly's wig is dislodged, and we see she is absolutely bald—another visual stunner. Of course we want to know the reason, and Fuller gives us the answer at the conclusion. Taking only the money that belongs to her, Kelly heads out of this unnamed Midwestern city, and we next see her in a small town, sitting on a park bench with her suitcase, looking at the local movie marquee, which is advertising *Shock Corridor*, another recent Fuller neo-noir. Kelly meets Griff (Anthony Eisley), a tough police captain who recognizes her for what she is. Using the guise of selling champagne, Kelly entices Griff into bed in his apartment; he lets her spend the night and then urges her to move on to work at Candy's Bon Bons, a house of prostitution that guarantees "indescribable pleasures." When Griff leaves, Kelly takes a long, hard look at herself in the mirror and realizes she wants to extricate herself from this kind of life completely. On Griff's wall she notices a framed news item and picture: "Grant Saves Griff in Korea: Wounded." Kelly leaves and rents a very pleasant room in the house of Miss Josephine (Betty Bronson); applies for a job to work with handicapped children in the local hospital, built by Grant's family; and embarks on a new life for herself. When Griff finds out from the local head nurse, Mac (played by longtime character actress Patsy Kelly), that Kelly is working at the hospital, he disparages her, believing an ex-hooker can never change.

But Kelly is a marvelous therapist for the handicapped children. There is a wonderful dream sequence to the song "The Bluebird" in which all of the crippled children are suddenly cured—"I have legs," one shouts—due to Kelly's nurturing and care. At a party given for the staff of the hospital at Grant's family estate, Kelly finally meets her sponsor/employer (played by Michael Dante). Apparently they both share a love for classical music, "Moonlight Sonata," Goethe, and Baudelaire. Kelly and Grant kiss on their second meeting in front of a roaring fireplace at his home, and she realizes something is wrong. They make love while watching his home movies taken on a recent vacation in Venice. Griff insinuates himself into Kelly's life, wanting to reveal the truth about her past to protect Grant. But Kelly confesses she told Grant everything about her.

There is a side plot involving one of the young, nubile nurses, Buff (played by Marie Devereux), whom Candy is trying to recruit as a prostitute. It seems Buff is pregnant and needs money for an abortion, but cannot obtain it on a nurse's salary, and so decides to sell "bonbons." When Kelly finds out about it, she goes to see Candy at her establishment across the river, and when they are alone, Kelly beats Candy (played harshly and very appropriately by Virginia Grey) with her handbag, forcing twenty-five dollars in bills into the latter's mouth, and warning her to leave Buff alone—a terrifically violent and unexpected scene.

Meanwhile, Grant asks Griff to be his best man and has given Kelly a key to his [their] home. Arriving one afternoon after shopping for her wedding dress and veil, Kelly surprises Grant as a nine-year-old girl skips out of the study after playing "games" with Uncle Grant. "Now you know why I can never marry a normal woman—that's why I love you—you understand my sickness—you're conditioned to people like me—our marriage will be a paradise—we're both abnormal." Kelly is so enraged by Grant's disclosure of his pedophilia that she clobbers him to death with a handy telephone receiver.

She is jailed for her crime, and the newspapers make good sport of the event. Headlines scream: "Grant Is Dead: Slain by Prostitute." Griff interrogates Kelly, discovers the meaning of "the naked kiss," and is told of Grant's perversity. Kelly reveals that a little girl was present in Grant's home, committing indecent acts with him, but Griff refuses to believe it unless Kelly can identify the little girl. Despite Kelly's good work at the hospital, the town condemns her for her past. Her former procurer arrives to testify against Kelly—it is revealed he got Kelly drunk and shaved her head because she forced six of his girls out on their own. Candy, the madam, also gives evidence against

Kelly, declaring, "Nobody forces dirty money into my mouth," even though her whole existence as a "stable-master" depends on "dirty money." Finally, Kelly does spot the little girl from her jail cell window, and, after an elaborate screening of all the town children, Kelly interviews the one child who played a "special" game with "Uncle Grant." Kelly is off the hook but is no longer on a pedestal. She leaves town alone exactly one year after her arrival, walking through the crowd of people waiting outside the jail. She bids goodbye to her landlady, but nobody stops her from leaving. Her fate is ambiguous, the film, open ended.

Fuller's neo-noir is basically about the abuse and exploitation of women, a theme never before handled so trenchantly in the 1960s. It is also an attack on the double standard exercised by men of this era—the male treatment of women is perverse. Fuller's film is full of taboo subjects—sexual deviancy, prostitution, small-town sanctimony and hypocrisy. His sensational tabloid background comes to a climax, full throttle in this unsubtle, scathing, nightmarish, almost surreal crime film. *The Naked Kiss* reveals darker secrets than we ever expected to see on the silver screen, but with no nuance or subtlety—only a sledgehammer rendering of outrageous truth in the Fuller neo-noir style.

5. POINT BLANK**** (1967)
99 minutes, Color

Director: John Boorman.
Producers: Judd Bernard, Irwin Winkler.
Screenplay: Alexander Jacobs, David Newhouse, Rafe Newhouse from the Richard Stark (Donald Westlake) novel *The Hunter.*
Photography: Philip H. Lathrop.
Music: Johnny Mandel.
Editing: Henry Berman.
Stars: Lee Marvin, Angie Dickinson, Keenan Wynn, Carroll O'Connor.
Metrocolor and CinemaScope. MGM/UA. VHS: Universal/MCA and MGM/UA, DVD: Criterion.

Point Blank is at the center of the neo-noir movement of the mid-1960s. It is a very, very violent film, starring Lee Marvin as Walker. It is also told in flashbacks. Walker is shot nearly dead by his very best friend, Mal Reese (played unctuously by John Vernon in his debut role), and his wife Lynn (Sharon Acker in her first screen role). Lynn betrayed Walker to Mal after they all participated in a very successful robbery on Alcatraz Island. But Walker is alive, seeking vengeance and his share of the proceeds from the robbery—ninety-three thousand dollars. He kills everyone who gets in his way, including mob kingpin Brewster (played by Carroll O'Conner), and threatens Angie Dickinson as Chris (Lynn's sister), the girl Mal took up with after he dropped Walker's wife because of her drug habit.

The real star of the film, however, is the city of Los Angeles. English director John Boorman uses the city locations effectively—getting the pace, architecture, even the odor of Los Angeles into his film. Some of the cutting is a bit convoluted as Lee Marvin triumphs over his would-be assassins only to lose out to the police. (Keenan Wynn plays an unscrupulous cop named Yost, after the mob and willing to use Walker.) The film is full of violence and sadism, typical of the new noir, and it also downplays any moral sense the characters may have once possessed. Lee Marvin as Walker is the antihero, a killer who must kill or be killed. But the film establishes one essential point: there is futility in revenge. Marvin plays his role as avenger to the hilt, mowing down anyone in his way in the inhumane, humorless, complex underworld of Los Angeles. His killing of Mal, his best friend, is particularly graphic, as he hurls the latter over a high balcony from a wrapped sheet to die naked and bloody in the street below. Walker is vicious, vengeful, and unstoppable.

However, he knows when to step back into the shadows and *not* take the money and run. Yost is out to kill his avenger, too.

Marvin gives the bravura performance of his life. No one can forget Marvin emptying his pistol in slow motion into a mob target or the sound of his footsteps running on pavement as he flashes back to similar criminal acts and anticipates future ones. The film has a simple, raw story that is told in a surreal fashion. It is tough and beautiful at the same time, with inspiring visuals and a deceptively annoying soundtrack; the film borders on hallucination or fantasy. It is not your usual linear noir rendition of love, murder, and revenge. It is one of the most stylized, arty thrillers ever made—with curiously angled cameras, fractured chronologies, and careful photographic compositions in each frame. Boorman uses the CinemaScope lens to perfection, making the Alcatraz locations absolutely cringe inducing with their closeness (for example, when Walker is left for dead in a cell). The Los Angeles highway bulges on its foundations as a hired gun (James Sikking) mistakenly picks off men from the "Organization" with his high-power rifle in the waterway below—a lonely and empty expanse of water and concrete.

The viewer gets no rest here—the visual and aural cues constantly stimulate to provide a complex, unnerving experience. The high point visually and aurally is Walker's revenge against Mal. From an apartment balcony, Mal is thrown from the right side of the screen to the left, divested of the sheet he was wrapped in, traveling down to the street, naked; the camera now peers over the edge like a god, to see his demise from above. Cut to Mal lying with a bloody face, head down, filling the center to the left side of the screen as passersby walk into the frame from the right, wondering what has happened. This is a brilliant use of the CinemaScope screen, and brilliant filmmaking!

It is too bad that Brian Helgeland tried to remake *Point Blank* in 1999 as *Payback*, starring Mel Gibson in the role of "Porter." Changing the name of our antihero to Porter and the setting to Chicago, the director of this neo-noir remake settles for a happy ending, some sadomasochism, and some physical cruelty. Like *Point Blank*, this film is not for the weak of heart—it is probably for the weak minded. *Payback* is more of an entertainment, with some cleverness in its execution of car chases and bombings. But it is totally artless. Boorman's great neo-noir *Point Blank* is artful, enticing, intellectually thrilling, mature stylistically, and the original neo-noir of true substance.

The Los Angeles locale is used terrifically once again in the digitally filmed 2004 Michael Mann production *Collateral*; just like Boorman's, Mann's views of the city vibrate with energy (see chapter 32).

6. DIRTY HARRY**** (1971)
102 minutes, Color

Director: Don Siegel.
Producer: Malpaso Productions (Clint Eastwood).
Screenplay: Harry Julian Fink, Rita M. Fink with Dean Reisner, John Milius (uncredited).
Photography: Bruce Surtees.
Music: Lalo Schifrin.
Editing: Carl Pingitore.
Stars: Clint Eastwood, Harry Guardino, Reni Santoni, John Vernon, Andy Robinson.
Technicolor and Panavision. Warner Bros. VHS & DVD: Warner Bros.

The 1970s ushered in a new type of noir film—the good/bad cop film that reinforced the trends of violence begun in the early 1960s. The 1970s saw the introduction of serial killers as protagonists; the loosening of censorship rules, permitting frontal female (and male) nudity on-screen; as well as the innovative use of location filming on CinemaScope or Panavision screens and in color. The detective/cop film took on a new look. It starred action heroes, like Clint Eastwood, who broke the rules and became vigilantes in their quest to maintain law and order in the big cities like San Francisco.

Dirty Harry is one of the best police movies or neo-noirs ever made. It took Clint Eastwood out of western garb and put him on the streets of San Francisco as detective inspector Harry Callahan, "dirty" because he likes absolutely nobody and is always the man to clean up the dirtiest situations. Harry is tall, anarchic, and cynical, and constantly delivers neat one-liners to resolve situations. When confronting criminals who try to shoot it out with him, he says, "Go ahead, make my day," waving his gigantic .44 Magnum in a threatening manner. Or he says, "Do you feel lucky?" as he addresses a criminal, who wonders whether Harry has emptied his entire gun or has one remaining bullet.

In the first of a series of four films, Harry Callahan is confronted by a psychotic sniper and serial killer called Scorpio. Scorpio kills nubile women in swimming pools, Catholics, and "niggers" while holding the city hostage, first for fifty thousand dollars and later for two million dollars and a jet plane in which to make his escape. The serial killer is played brilliantly by blue-eyed Andy Robinson, who gets away with multiple murders the first time because of an illegal gun search of his apartment and also because Det. Callahan fails to "read him his rights." Scorpio has buried a young woman alive, and Callahan is determined to learn her whereabouts before the young woman suffocates. In a breathtaking scene, Callahan traps Scorpio in the middle of a football field, shooting him in the leg. Scorpio insists on his rights, but Callahan applies pressure to the wound, forcing Scorpio to scream violently as the camera swoops backward and up, outside of the stadium, the screams becoming muffled in the distance. The mayor (capably played by John Vernon) and the police chief (John Larch) advise Harry of the consequences of not observing the Miranda Law and tell him Scorpio will be out on the streets of San Francisco again. The lawmen believe this is the end of Scorpio's reign of terror, but Harry tells them, "He'll do it again because he likes to kill."

An interesting sadomasochistic aside takes place when Scorpio pays a black man to beat him up badly, trying to frame Harry Callahan for brutality. It does not work, but it gets Harry off his trail for the time being. However, Scorpio is just a plain psychopath and abducts a school bus filled with children and the driver, telephoning the mayor for another ransom payment. Harry shows up on the side of the road, jumps on top of the bus, throttles Scorpio, and seriously wounds him. Scorpio plays his last hand out, believing Harry has no bullets—but Harry shoots him dead with the last bullet in his .44 Magnum, blowing his body off into a local river. Harry looks down at the corpse, takes out his badge, and hurls it far into the river past the floating body. "The End."

Clearly, detective inspector Harry Callahan cannot follow the rules. When he tosses his badge into the river, he reaffirms his spirit of vigilantism. Harry cannot exist in a society filled with evil. His wife was killed in a freak auto accident when a drunken driver crossed the median, causing a head-on collision. Harry survived her death and continues his fight for survival in the city. The director, Don Siegel, lovingly photographs Mount Davison Park and other San Francisco landmarks with a gritty realism; in these scenes, Harry triumphs over the geographical spectacle. Siegel uses masterful helicopter shots and wide-angle lensing to advantage, letting Harry dominate the frame in his battle for survival over San Francisco's lowlifes. One feels the director is on Harry's side as he struggles for law and order, sometimes outside of the rules. Excessive force is the rule; Harry likes to shoot first and ask questions later. Certainly *Dirty Harry* is one of the best of the new noirs of its decade. All of the sequels—*Magnum Force* (1973), *The Enforcer* (1976), *Sudden Impact* (1983), and *The Dead Pool* (1988)—may have been commercially successful, but do not have the impact of the original *Dirty Harry*.

7. THE FRENCH CONNECTION**** (1971)
104 minutes, Color by Deluxe

Director: William Friedkin.
Producer: Philip D'Antoni.
Screenplay: Ernest Tidyman, Robin Moore, based on Moore's novel.
Photography: Owen Roizman.
Music: Don Ellis.
Editing: Jerry Greenberg.
Stars: Gene Hackman, Roy Scheider, Fernando Rey, Tony Lo Bianco.
Color by Deluxe, CinemaScope. 20th Century Fox. VHS & DVD: Fox.

Philip D'Antoni made the most exciting police film in 1968, *Bullitt*, starring Steve McQueen and featuring one of the best movie car-chase scenes ever filmed. D'Antoni tops this film with *The French Connection*, which has earned its place in the sun as one of the best new noir/cop action films ever made. It won the Academy Award for Best Picture of 1971, as well as Oscars for Gene Hackman (as Popeye Doyle), its screenplay, and Jerry Greenberg's editing.

The film was shot on location in Manhattan and Brooklyn and is based on a true case in which sixty kilos of heroin were seized by New York police, found in the "rockers" of a Lincoln Continental delivered from Marseilles. Ernest Tidyman fashioned a wonderful screenplay from Robin Moore's story about this true crime case and even starred as one of the cops in the film—Eddie Egan played another role (and acted as an advisor on the film). Gene Hackman has the role of his life as a vulgar, brutal, tireless, unlikable, maniacal, and sadistic Jimmy Doyle. With his partner, Buddy Russo (unflinchingly played by Roy Scheider), Doyle obsessively and passionately tracks down the French drug pushers and makes the largest narcotics seizure by New York police in the early 1960s.

The film begins in Marseilles, where a hit man for the French mob, Pierre Nicoli (played by Marcel Bozzuffi), shoots a French detective in the face and eats a piece of his baguette after committing the murder. At approximately the same time, Doyle, dressed in a Santa Claus outfit, and Russo, as a hot dog vendor, chase a knife-wielding dope pusher into a local bar. They see large sums of money being flashed by Sal Boca (terrifically played by Tony Lo Bianco), a small-time candy store owner whose legitimate yearly income is much less than what he spends daily around town. Assuming Sal and Angie's Candy Store is a drug drop, Doyle and Russo get permission from their police captain to have a wire placed in the candy store. Continuing their surveillance, they follow Sal into Manhattan, to the apartment of a Jewish drug kingpin named Joel Weinstock (Harold Gary), who is backing a scheme to import heroin from Marseilles.

Further surveillance leads the team of detectives to Alain Charnier (played wonderfully by Spanish actor Fernando Rey) and his hit man, Nicoli. In Marseilles, the two drug dealers have hired Henri Devereux, an actor/producer in need of money, to take their Lincoln Continental (loaded with heroin, unbeknownst to Devereux) into New York. When Weinstock, Boca, and Charnier meet up, Doyle and Russo know they are on to something big!

The rest of the film is a police procedural. It shows how narcotic agents uncover the hidden heroin and how Doyle and Russo track the criminals relentlessly—suffering in the winter cold eating pizza while Charnier and Nicoli have an elegant lunch at the Champlain Restaurant, following them into and out of hotels and onto planes to Washington DC, and back.

There are two wonderful set pieces in the film. The first is a game Charnier and Doyle play on the subway: Charnier (Rey) suspects Doyle is following him and pops in and out of a subway car, Doyle following suit. Finally Charnier uses his umbrella to force open a closing subway door, then pops back into the train; Doyle is left running after him on the platform as the train pulls away, with Charnier coyly smiling and waving goodbye. The most thrilling part of the film is the chase by Doyle in a borrowed car as the subway train proceeds nonstop overhead on an elevated portion of track (probably MacDonald Avenue in Brooklyn). Nicoli, the French hit man, has just tried to kill Doyle at his low-income apartment house in Brooklyn, taking careful aim with a rifle but missing him. Doyle climbs to the roof and sees Nicoli running in the streets below. Doyle gives chase, and Nicoli catches an uptown local train. Doyle commandeers a local citizen's car and begins to chase the runaway train. Aboard the train Nicoli kills first a policeman then a transit guard. The motorman has a heart attack and crashes his train into the rear of one stopped at a local station. Below, Doyle has followed the train, almost colliding with a mother and a child in a carriage. As Nicoli comes down the stairs from the train, Doyle awaits him, gun in hand. Nicoli refuses to surrender, so Doyle shoots him in the back (the most famous image of the film, seen in its poster art), and Nicoli falls backward down the stairs to his death. Breathtaking!

In the finale, the police close in on the criminals on Wards Island (a garbage dump where Boca's brother (another accomplice) works. Boca is killed trying to shoot it out with the police, Weinstock is arrested, and Charnier slips away as Doyle fires aimlessly into an empty subterranean warehouse. Doyle's bullets accidentally hit Mulderig (Bill Hickman), who has been riding Doyle about another cop getting killed because of Doyle's ineptitude. The film ends with a series of titles about the criminals and the cops: Joel Weinstock was indicted, but his case was dismissed for lack of evidence; Angie Boca received a suspended sentence for a misdemeanor; Lou Boca received a reduced sentence, guilty of conspiracy; Henri Devereux served four years in a federal prison, guilty of conspiracy (the dupe of Charnier); and Alain Charnier was never caught, but is believed to be living in France. Doyle says at the end of the film after mistakenly killing Mulderig: "I'm gonna get him. I saw him. The son of a bitch is here. I saw him." Detectives Doyle and Russo were transferred out of the Narcotics Bureau and reassigned elsewhere.

The French Connection is gritty, raw, neo-noir filmmaking at its best. It captures the seedy ambience of drug dealers in Brooklyn bars and the colloquial language of criminals and detectives always on the edge. As in Point Blank (1967), you can smell New York City and feel the cold in the vivid locations shot by photographer Owen Roizman, who uses a naturalistic camera eye. French Connection II (1973) tries to tie up the loose ends of the original, even resurrecting Charnier as a movie character and sending Popeye Doyle to Marseilles, where he gets hooked on drugs. But the sequel is merely a staged attempt to recreate the original, and it meets with little success. Fox and John Frankenheimer should have known better than to have Doyle pursue Charnier in France, which in reality never occurred. The original French Connection has the imprint of truth and the uncomfortable ring of open-ended reality. In life, some criminals do escape, and the new noir supports that notion rather than a conveniently neat ending.

8. CHINATOWN**** (1974)
131 minutes, Color

Director: Roman Polanski.
Producer: Robert Evans.
Screenplay: Robert Towne.
Photography: John A. Alonzo.
Music: Jerry Goldsmith.
Editing: Sam O'Steen.
Stars: Jack Nicholson, Faye Dunaway, John Huston, Perry Lopez, John Hillerman.
Technicolor and Panavision. Paramount. VHS & DVD: Paramount (in letterbox version).

Chinatown is the most perfect example of a neo-noir film (up to the appearance of Curtis Harrington's *L.A. Confidential* in 1997). Its time frame is the late 1930s (1937 to be exact), but it is a new noir because it offers keener, more contemporary psychological insights into its characters than noir films made in that era. Nothing has escaped the perception of writer Robert Towne, who has spun a private-eye story about Jake Gittes (expertly played by Jack Nicholson), who, while investigating a case of adultery, stumbles onto a murder scheme that has something to do with water rights and incest in the city of Los Angeles. Gittes is a private dick who is intelligent, charismatic, and completely tactless. Set up to investigate a simple case of adultery, he finds himself led into an ever darkening world of family intrigue and political and moral corruption on a grand scale. When *Chinatown* was released in 1974, it was immediately thought of as belonging to the neo-noir style of filmmaking—it has the essentially lonely antihero, the detective, looking into other people's secrets while escaping from his own; it has the femme fatale (a gorgeous Faye Dunaway as Evelyn Mulwray) who almost leads Gittes to his destruction through her sexuality; it has layers and layers of mysterious, intertwining plot twists; and finally, it has a surprising noir denouement in which evil triumphs over good. If film critics blur the history of film noir and its successor, neo-noir, it is almost possible to place *Chinatown* in the pantheon of great noir films—a glorious testament to its story, direction, setting, and style—and in color and CinemaScope, too.

The screenplay of *Chinatown*, written by Robert Towne, is partially based on the true story of the Owens River Valley scandal of 1908. Set in Los Angeles in 1937, the film pays homage to the best films noirs of Raymond Chandler and Dashiell Hammett. It begins as a crimer but ends metaphorically, in the real world of Chinatown, where you never know what you are dealing with and you meet a tragic end. Perhaps reflecting the cynicism of the Watergate era, which is very new noir, *Chinatown* interweaves puzzles about a water-related land grab and a family mired in sexual dysfunction.

We first meet Jake Gittes in his office, talking to a client whose wife has been committing adultery. Jake employs two men to gather evidence, incriminating photographs, and recordings to document the wayward affairs of rich spouses. His next client, "Mrs. Mulwray" (really Ida Sessions, played by Diane Ladd—a dupe to incriminate Mr. Mulwray) pays Jake to investigate her "husband" and take photos of any indiscretions. Hollis Mulwray (Darrell Zwerling) is the chief engineer of the Los Angeles Water and Power Company and is supposedly having a dalliance with a teenage girl. Jake's snoops photograph Mulwray fondling and kissing an unknown blonde in a rowboat in Echo Park. He gives the photos to "Mrs. Mulwray" and discovers the next day, to his utter surprise, that the photos have been printed in the newspaper!

On the following day, the "real" Mrs. Mulwray (Faye Dunaway) visits Gittes's office and threatens to sue him for defaming her husband's character. Obviously, the detective was duped by someone who hired a woman to pose as Mrs. Mulwray to damage Mr. Mulwray's reputation. Gittes goes to see Mr. Mulwray first at his office, later at his home to apologize and avoid a lawsuit. At this time in Los Angeles, there is a terrible drought, and Gittes notices the Mulwray's gardener is watering their pool garden with salt water. Jake also notices something shining at the bottom of that very same pool, a clue that will have future significance. Not finding Mr. Mulwray again, Jake visits with Mrs. Mulwray, who suddenly is eager to drop her lawsuit, telling Gittes her husband is probably at Oak Pass or the Stone Canyon Reservoir.

Jake makes his way to Oak Pass, then the reservoir, where the body of Hollis Mulwray is found—he is apparently an accidental drowning victim in the middle of a drought! Investigating further, Jake discovers another victim of a drowning—a drunk who lived in the storm drains of Los Angeles. Suspicious, Jake returns one evening to the Oak Pass Reservoir and is caught in a violent rush of water that slams him into the fence of a storm drain. Extricating himself over the fence he is then fired on by Claude Mulvihill, Mulwray's deputy commissioner, who also has two thugs in his employ. One of them (played by director Roman Polanski) tells Jake to stop nosing around and with a knife viciously slits one of Jake's nostrils. But Jake's curiosity cannot be stopped. He returns to Mrs. Mulwray's mansion and accuses her of hiding something. He also finds out that Evelyn C. Mulwray is the daughter of land and power tycoon Noah Cross (excellently played by John Huston), who *owned* the Water Department.

Evelyn finally reveals that her husband and father had a falling out over the ownership of the water, and Jake visits Noah Cross at the Albacore Club. Cross then hires Jake to find the teenager smitten with Hollis Mulwray, and another mysterious layer to the film begins to evolve. Gittes discovers widespread political corruption and dirty land grab deals made by Cross. He has bought up farmland and in fact the entire valley; he irrigates only the lands that are profitable to his enterprises, especially orange groves. Hollis Mulwray was killed, apparently, because he opposed the building of a reservoir that was part of Cross's scheme of power.

There are numerous plot twists and turns in the last hour of the film, but the most significant scenes deal with Gittes's realization that he is a victim of Noah Cross's schemes as well as a key player in the tragic conclusion. After Gittes has various skirmishes with the thugs who work for the deputy commissioner, Evelyn Mulwray saves Gittes from another beating, rushing him away in her car. He is grateful to her for this and her care of his cut nose, and they finally become intimate. In the new noir style, both Gittes and Mulwray are shown naked in bed, smoking cigarettes after making love. Talking about his past, he reveals to her how he tried to save a woman he loved in Chinatown ("where you can't tell what's going on") and how his interference hastened her tragic demise. Here screenwriter Robert Towne and director Roman Polanski are using a bit of cinematic foreshadowing; Gittes's insistence on solving the mystery might be Evelyn Mulwray's undoing.

Evelyn warns Jake about how dangerous her father is. She also reveals the identity of the teenager, Katherine: "She's my sister." They both discover from police lieutenant Lou Escobar (wonderfully played by Perry Ellis) that Hollis was murdered. He had salt water in his lungs. Jake then finds Hollis's glasses at the bottom of the salt-water pool garden, and it is at this point that Evelyn reveals the true identity of the girl she has been sheltering—"She's my sister *and* my daughter." Apparently, Noah Cross had incestuous relations with his daughter—a layer of the mystery that parallels Cross's violation of Los Angeles county land, the corruption of the water department, the building of the new reservoir, the land swindle. Evelyn wants to spirit her daughter away from her incestuous father (to Mexico by car). It is also revealed the glasses in the bottom of the pool are bifocals belonging to Noah Cross, *not* Hollis Mulwray. And so Gittes visits Cross one last time in the hope of stopping the tycoon from committing more crimes against his family and the city. Cross is far above Gittes's petty concerns. He tells Jake about a new dam he intends to build to irrigate the valley and how he envisages Los Angeles becoming one huge metropolitan area. Murder and incest hardly matter to a visionary like Noah Cross! Gittes asks Cross, "How much better can you eat? What can you buy that you can't already afford?" Cross replies: "The future, Mr. 'Gits,' the future. Now where's the girl? I want the only daughter I've got left."

It is in Chinatown that all the strands of the plot and the characters in the film converge. Evelyn and her daughter/sister have been staying with the family of their Chinese butler and are ready to leave for Mexico when Gittes leads Cross to their hideout. Cross threatens Evelyn, intimating that he will have incestuous relations with Katherine, but Evelyn threatens her father with a gun and drives off with her daughter into the crowded Chinatown streets. After Evelyn wounded her father in the arm when he tried to prevent her departure, Lt. Escobar fires his gun into the air, a warning for Evelyn to stop the car. She refuses, and Escobar fires four more shots, one of them into the head of Evelyn as the car rolls to a stop. Cross takes his sobbing daughter, horrified by her mother's death and disfigured head, into his car. Jake is devastated. Cross has triumphed, and Gittes realizes he has caused the death of another woman he loved—and once again, in Chinatown. Escobar tells Jake to go home and lays the blame on Chinatown, which has a foreign ambience and is a place where everything inexplicable happens. "Forget it, Jake. It's Chinatown." Jake cannot forget the multiple tragedies—and his participation in the events that have caused Noah Cross to triumph politically (and sexually, as a deviant) and the loss of his second love, Evelyn. The camera pulls back as the police order everyone to clear the streets of Chinatown. End title. The Los Angeles newspaper would probably report the death of Evelyn in a shootout in Chinatown in one of a group of articles about events that take place there almost every day. Here is where the significance of the title comes into play: people come and go in Chinatown, but nothing worthwhile really happens! But the audience of this film certainly knows better.

As Byzantine as its plot is, *Chinatown* is a great new noir. Like most noir films of that style, it ends in a downbeat way and with a flurry of revelations. Also, by casting John Huston in the role of the villain, Noah Cross, Polanski connects his *Chinatown* to the eruption of 1940s noir; John Huston was both screenwriter and director of *The Maltese Falcon*, one of the signposts of the beginning of American noir style. What better resonance than casting John Huston, a 1940s icon, in a new noir film! Moreover, Polanski's *Chinatown* transcends the old noir to become one of the best meditations on the bottomless well of human mystery, corruption, and sexuality, as well as a definitive masterpiece of the new noir era.

One last note: Its sequel, *The Two Jakes* (1990), directed by Nicholson, was an artistic disaster. It resurrected some of the original plot motifs, but to minor effect.

9. NIGHT MOVES*** (1975)
99 minutes, Color

Director: Arthur Penn.
Producer: Robert M. Sherman.
Screenplay: Alex Sharp.
Photography: Bruce Surtees.
Music: Michael Small.
Editing: Dede Allen.
Stars: Gene Hackman, Jennifer Warren, Susan Clark, Edward Binns, Melanie Griffith.
Technicolor. Warner Bros. VHS: Warners.

Night Moves is a new noir that follows the patterns of the film noir of the 1940s and 1950s. Gene Hackman plays a former footballer, Harry Moseby, who now earns his living as a private investigator for the rich and famous in Hollywood. (Compare this with Taylor Hackford's *Against All Odds* (1984), with Jeff Bridges in a practically identical situation.) Harry is hired by ex–movie star Arlene Iverson (Janet Ward) to find her errant stepdaughter, Delly (Melanie Griffith in her first screen role). It seems Delly has run off to the Florida Keys, and her mother, now married to a movie mogul, wants her back. Delly wants to remain in Florida with her father, Tom Iverson (played by John Crawford), and has no intention of returning unless Harry Moseby brings her back by force. Delly's stepmother wants her back only so that she can control her daughter's trust fund and suggests to Harry that her ex-husband has lured Delly to Florida.

Plot complications arise when Harry becomes enmeshed in a Florida smuggling ring involving Iverson and his mistress, Paula (beautifully played by the very much underrated Jennifer Warren). Harry is divorced from his wife, Ellen (played by Susan Clark), who is currently having an affair with stalwart and stable Marty Heller (Harris Yulin in one of his good guy roles). Illicit sex is dangled in front of Harry by a nude and youthful Delly (so he won't take her back to her mother) and also by Paula, with whom Harry does finally fall into a blazing affair. Paula's dalliance serves to divert Harry's attention from her husband's drug smuggling activities.

Tied to the Florida plot is an unsolved Hollywood murder in the world of stuntmen and a suspicious mechanic named Quentin (James Woods, also in his first film role). It seems Harry has enough on his mind, trying to solve his own marital problems as well as crack the covered-up murder case. He eventually discovers that Joey Ziegler (played by character actor Ed Binns), a former stuntman who is head of a Yucatan-based ring smuggling Colombian artifacts, used Iverson, his wife, and their Florida home as an entry point to sell these priceless objects. So what begins as a mere tracing of a runaway teenager becomes a convoluted, labyrinthine mystery that turns out disastrously for Harry at the end.

One day, while swimming near her father's fishing cabin in the Florida Keys, Delly discovers the plane and body of her runaway pilot-stuntman lover, with whom she had been living briefly on a film location in the southwest. Harry had tracked her there but later caught up with Delly in Florida. Seeing her lover dead, Delly agrees to return to Los Angeles with Harry. But the very next day, Delly is killed while filming a movie stunt. This is too coincidental for Harry; he watches the footage of the "accident" repeatedly and becomes convinced she was murdered. Harry has an obsessive need to know the truth. Returning to the Florida Keys, Harry is convinced he will find the answer to Delly's murder there. He discovers that Tom Iverson and his lover, Paula, have committed several murders in the interim to cover up their smuggling of pre-Colombian art into the United States. Harry discovers the entire operation, fights and chases the smugglers, and shoots down their seaplane in a spectacular crash. Harry has been wounded by gunfire and is left stranded, standing alone in a motorboat, watching the plane sink into the ocean as his boat makes ever-widening circles. Harry has discovered the truth, but it has left him desolate, impotent, alone. He will probably never get together with his wife, since everything now seems futile to him. Yes, Harry Moseby solved the crime, but he was not smart enough to see his own place in the world and triumph over his personal failings.

Besides Gene Hackman (who has mellowed a bit since his role of Popeye Doyle in William Friedkin's *The French Connection*, made just a few years before), Jennifer Warren is the only actor to give a terrific performance in the film. She comes alive as Iverson's sometime mistress and Harry's short-term lover. It is too bad she did not receive better roles after *Night Moves*. *Night Moves* is another succès d'estime for director Arthur Penn, most famous for his *Bonnie and Clyde* (1967). Unfortunately, most motion picture critics lambasted *Night Moves*, seeing it as two different stories joined together—a murder/mayhem mystery combined with the story of a detective confronting his own failed life. But it is precisely this melding of stories that makes *Night Moves* a most unusual new noir. Harry Moseby is a man with limitations and weaknesses, a new dimension for detectives of the 1970s. Gone are the Philip Marlowes and tough-guy private investigators who have tremendous insights into crime and can triumph over criminals because they carry within them a code of honor. Harry cannot fathom what honor is, much less be subsumed by it. He is adrift in an existential world, lost, alone, vulnerable. Where Sam Spade sent femme fatale Brigid O'Shaunessy to the rigors of prison at Tehachape, Harry was seduced by Paula, who used him and would have caused his total downfall if she had not been brutally murdered herself. *Night Moves* certainly is new noir, with many twists and turns in its plot and a complexity to its characters that would defy even psychoanalysis. This makes it a fascinating new noir.

10. TAXI DRIVER**** (1976)
113 minutes, Color

Director: Martin Scorsese.
Producers: Julia Philips, Michael Phillips.
Screenplay: Paul Schrader.
Photography: Michael Chapman.
Music: Bernard Herrmann.
Editors: Tom Rolf, Melvin Shapiro.
Stars: Robert De Niro, Cybill Shepherd, Peter Boyle, Jodie Foster, Harvey Keitel, Albert Brooks.
Metrocolor and Wide Screen. Columbia Pictures. VHS & DVD: Columbia.

As we enter the latter part of the 1970s, Martin Scorsese's film *Taxi Driver* is the first one to depart from the detective mode of neo-noir and introduce the theme of the existential alienation of soldiers who participated in the Vietnam War. Clearly, Scorsese's film, based on Paul Schrader's mind-boggling script, is strong stuff—in fact, in a recent restoration of the film, the director had to agree to use sepia over the violent conclusion to tone down the graphically explicit murders in order to obtain an R rating instead of an X, which would have been anathema at the box office. Scorsese wants his masterwork to be seen even in this truncated form, for *Taxi Driver* has much to offer in the way of performances, script, dialogue, story line, and societal metaphors.

Taxi Driver is the story of Travis Bickle (played with enormous strength and sensitivity by Robert De Niro), a Vietnam veteran who finds that life in the United States has been turned upside down for him when he returns to New York City. He cannot sleep and experiences a great sense of isolation from his fellow New Yorkers. So he takes a job driving a taxi at night, when he can make the most money, despite the danger—and get paid for his insomnia. The fares he picks up are usually lowlifes, repugnant on every level—pimps, prostitutes, johns, and adulterous husbands. Regarding the latter, he picks up Martin Scorsese (in a cameo role), who has Travis park by an apartment building as they both gaze up at a window where his unfaithful wife is having sex with a "nigger"; Scorsese's character relates to Travis how he is going to get revenge, blowing both of them away with his .44 Magnum. Scorsese has been the critical object of feminists ever since he filmed that scene. Bickle also talks in a voice-over about how he has to clean the back of his cab nightly to get rid of the cum, the sleaze, the blood! Travis accepts the dregs of society and goes to any destination at any time. (One should note this film was made twenty years before the rash of taxi driver assassinations that culminated in greater police surveillance and harsher punishments for perpetrators.)

On the brighter side, Travis meets Betsy (played by Cybill Shepherd), a political aide to Charles Palantine (played by broadcaster Leonard Harris), and accepts her as a fare in his large checker cab. Betsy is a cool customer, trying to get Travis to commit as a volunteer for Palantine. All Travis wants to do is date her and commits his greatest blunder when he takes her to a porno double feature at a sleazy theater on 42nd Street. (In the late 1990s, 42nd Street underwent a great renaissance, filling with new cinemas, restaurants, and legitimate theaters; pimps, prostitutes, drug dealers, and other undesirables were booted out. The 42nd Street of *Taxi Driver* exists only in Scorsese's film.)

Clearly Travis has no social skills, and Betsy drops him like a hot potato. He sends her flowers and cards, all of which are returned to his dingy studio apartment, where the flowers rot. On another venture into communicating with the opposite sex, Travis picks up Iris (wonderfully played by Jodie Foster), a teenage prostitute (she may be twelve years old, says her pimp, Sport, played by Harvey Keitel). Travis, like a knight in shining armor, tries to help Iris flee from Sport's influence, but Iris has nowhere to go—she says her family in Pittsburgh absolutely hates her! Having no success with either Betsy or Iris, Travis retreats into his lonely mode and starts to buy an assortment of guns, including a .44 Magnum. He begins to "train" for his new job: to assassinate Charles Palantine, the candidate for whom Betsy is working.

Insinuating himself at a rally, Travis makes small talk to a Secret Service agent who realizes he is dangerous—but Travis has no opportunity to unleash his wrath at the rally. Instead, he goes downtown to the Soho area, where he meets up with Sport, who insists on keeping Iris in his stable. Travis shoots Sport in the stomach and blows away a mafioso who had been taking a payoff from the pimp, as well as the hotel (brothel) manager. He frees Iris from her captors. Travis is shot at and wounded twice. Scorsese photographs this bloodbath in an overhead tracking shot (now covered in sepia tone). Instead of being arrested for murder, Travis instantly becomes a media hero.

Back on the job with his coterie of taxi driver pals, Travis gains some sort of adulation from them and his public. Even Betsy becomes interested in him again, but he ultimately rejects her. Without accepting her fare, he drives off into the night, into a world of sleaze and loneliness, into an uncertain tomorrow. Travis is to be pitied, not lionized. He is a victim of the Vietnam War; he has been disconnected, alienated from American society and carries a psychosis within him that may erupt in the future into mass murder. When Travis looks in a mirror, armed to the teeth, he says to himself, "You talking to me?" daring anyone to get in his way. Obviously, everyone has been talking "at" Travis, not "to" him, which has caused a huge gap in communication on his repatriation from Vietnam. Perhaps Scorsese and Schrader are saying that violence may be a precondition for Travis's reentry into American society. Or it is hopeless for anyone to break free of a confused, morally corrupt world, in which loneliness and commercialism are the operating factors, not love or compassion for the human spirit.

Perhaps Schrader and Scorsese are criticizing the decadent world of the United States of the 1970s—expressing their cynicism about the Watergate scandal, their disenchantment with the Vietnam War, their rejection of the American political system. *Taxi Driver* is a film about urban alienation and the workings of the alienated mind, snapped into a miasma of gory violence. (The film did not cause the violence of Columbine or Seattle, but perhaps predicted these massacres.)

Apropos of reality, much has been made of John Hinckley Jr.'s attempt to assassinate president Ronald Reagan, stemming from Hinckley's fascination with the Jodie Foster character and the film *Taxi Driver*. Scorsese created an artistic masterpiece, not a blueprint for murder. If a person like Hinckley merged the worlds of fantasy and reality, he must be clinically insane. Even Hinckley admitted that he developed a fantasy life based on this film—but that is certainly a problem concerning his own mental health and stability. Scorsese feels he can ignore the boundary between fantasy and reality *in film*, not in life.

Taxi Driver even today remains a masterful psychological study of an unbalanced soul who reverts to complete insanity, but winds up as a media hero at the conclusion. We never know if he has changed or will revert to violence in his own claustrophobic world. When Travis dons the Mohawk haircut, we know his mind has snapped completely. The "real rain, . . . to wash all the scum off the streets" is the bloodbath he inflicts at the film's conclusion. Travis has taken his violence beyond any fantasy world he has, perhaps as a result of his existential loneliness. Travis is a tortured, obsessive soul, looking for a new life, a new identity, as a savior of child prostitutes or a political assassin, to right all the wrongs of the world—unemployment, inflation, crime, corruption, war, pestilence, and so on. Travis returns to his violent nature as an insanely destructive means of achieving his own cathartic salvation.

The photographer, Michael Chapman, has to be given praise for his uniquely grainy, realistic photography—almost like tabloid photography that has a hard, lurid look. Composer Bernard Herrmann's score for the film contains a plaintive, jazzy riff that undulates with the violence and the sophistication of the burgeoning New York metropolis. Schrader's script is certainly on target, a critical treatise that has surreal components about America of the 1970s. His realistic dialogue, especially as spoken by the pimp, Sport, is so graphic and lurid that one winces from its realist bite. Peter Boyle as Wizard, one of Travis's fellow cab drivers, gives a terrific performance as a narcissistic, sleazy operator in a world of nighttime despair. His monologue to the drivers about a backseat seduction is priceless machismo. *Taxi Driver* is probably one of the best American films of the 1970s. It is a new noir classic that combines all the elements of its predecessors—film noir, the horror film (bloodbath scene), the Western (Travis's shoot-em-up scenes), and black-and-white urban melodramas with a noirish style, like *Kiss of Death* (1947), *The Naked City* (1948), *Cry of the City* (1949), and *The Asphalt Jungle* (1950). All of these noirish films present a harrowing portrait of man's alienation and loneliness in New York and other urban settings, but Martin Scorsese's *Taxi Driver* is the most superb, disturbing, gritty, nightmarish color classic; it is the best neo-noir of them all.

11. BODY HEAT**** (1981)
118 minutes, Color

Director: Lawrence Kasdan.
Producer: Fred T. Gallo.
Screenplay: Lawrence Kasdan.
Photography: Richard H. Kline.
Music: John Barry.
Editing: Carol Littleton.
Stars: William Hurt, Kathleen Turner, Richard Crenna, Ted Danson, Mickey Rourke.
Technicolor and CinemaScope. Warner Bros. VHS & DVD: Warners.

Body Heat is the best example of a neo-noir film derived from the great James M. Cain novel of the 1930s, *Double Indemnity*, which goes unacknowledged in the screenwriting credits. The original screenplay for Billy Wilder's 1944 film was coscripted by the director himself and Raymond Chandler, the great pulp mystery writer of the 1930s and 1940s, both of whom made *Double Indemnity* into a classic film noir. *Body Heat* is Chandler's *Double Indemnity*, revived, because of the easing of censorship codes, with explicit sex scenes.

The fundamental story of *Body Heat* has significant parallels with its predecessor. A dazzlingly attractive and sensual woman (Kathleen Turner as Matty Walker), for love *and* money, uses her wits and sexuality to ensnare a weak-willed, easily dominated (and manipulated) male (William Hurt as Ned Racine), whom she convinces to murder her nebbish of a husband (Richard Crenna as Edmund Walker). Of course, the deluded male is tricked and ends up with neither the money nor the dame, impotent, and in prison, too. He knows Matty planned for him to murder the real Matty Walker (called Mary Ann in the film) and has to serve out his prison sentence before he can do anything about it. Out of jealousy, he has a low-life criminal set a bomb that supposedly will kill his lover Matty. What Ned does not know is that the real Matty Walker (Mary Ann) is already dead. The imposter Matty kills her offscreen and places her body in the gazebo, the site of the explosion. When Ned receives Matty's yearbook in the mail, he realizes Matty Walker and Mary Ann had reversed identities but is helpless to catch the real murderer.

In *Double Indemnity*, it is Fred MacMurray, cast against type, playing a somewhat cute but dim insurance agent, who is entangled by the teasing, blonde, anklet-wearing housewife Barbara Stanwyck. She wants him to kill her husband in a scheme that involves a "railroad accident" and would net her a double indemnity insurance payment.

The women in both movies are apparently trapped in loveless marriages, seeking to dissolve their unions through profitable murders. Both women are also very, very greedy—they want to manipulate their lovers and reap their husband's fortunes.

What makes *Double Indemnity* a fabulous example of the noir style is that as dictated by the movie production codes of the era, jealousy sets into Fred MacMurray's relationship with Barbara Stanwyck after they both commit murder. Believing Stanwyck has another, much younger lover, MacMurray murders her out of a jealous revenge, and he probably bleeds to death from a shot returned by the dying Stanwyck.

In the updated story of *Body Heat*, a true neo-noir, William Hurt is manipulated by a shrewd Kathleen Turner into a position of culpability and capital punishment. Hurt is imprisoned for killing Richard Crenna. He believes Turner died in a bombing incident he helped to set up, with Mickey Rourke planting the bomb, to get rid of a potential witness—the real Matty Walker. The Kasdan script trumps the original Chandler scenario by killing off a substitute character, Turner's best friend, and having the black widow flee to some exotic land with her husband's fortune. Meanwhile, the murderer, Ned Racine, realizes too late, while in jail, that he has been the dupe, the true victim of a very, very unscrupulous and sinister woman. We also see throughout the film that Ned is a very incompetent lawyer; he makes changes in Edmund Walker's will that are subject to question and that allow Matty to grab her husband's total fortune. (In reality, half of it should have gone to Edmund's niece, Heather—a point of law in which the director erred.)

In 1980s neo-noir, the male characters are far more vulnerable. In the 1940s films, male protagonists are a lot simpler; sex (off screen) and money are their only objectives. Compare Fred MacMurray of *Double Indemnity* and Burt Lancaster in Robert Siodmak's *Criss Cross* (1949) or Siodmak's earlier noir classic *The Killers* (1946). Both men are naive and vulnerable, and they die because they are trapped unsuspectingly by vicious spider-women— femmes fatales like Stanwyck, Yvonne de Carlo, and Ava Gardner. Also, in 1940s noir, the plots are less tortuous. In 1980s neo-noir, there are convolutions and plot twists that dazzle and leave the audience limp and breathless. During the 1930s and 1940s, crime did not pay, and punishment was meted out accordingly. (For example, in a scene cut from the original 1944 *Double Indemnity*, we watch Fred MacMurray as Walter Neff die in the gas chamber at San Quentin.) From the late 1950s through the 1990s, the rules governing morality drastically changed. World War II, McCarthyism, and the Watergate scandal all caused a kind of decadence that destroyed the American dream. Consequently, the portrayal of American society in films, especially relationships between men and women, deteriorated and changed drastically after the 1960s and 1970s. Obviously the 1980s femme fatale triumphs in *Body Heat*. She gets the money, and she may hunt for another male victim. (Watch Theresa Russell in Bob Rafelson's 1987 film *Black Widow*.) Ned Racine's betrayal is a classic, pure noir experience because we, the audience, participate in his downfall as we watch it. When Matty Walker (Turner) says to Ned Racine (Hurt), "You're not too smart, are you? I like that in a man," she really means it. She picks up Ned, seduces him at her home (remember those jingling wind chimes?), takes him to bed on silk sheets, and then bathes with him in the nude as he complains, "I'm red. I'm sore. You shouldn't wear that body!"

Several factors make *Body Heat* a true neo-noir: the use of color and CinemaScope, that the femme fatale is cleverer than the male every step of the way, and that she triumphs masterfully! And all that sexual dialogue! She says, "Do it! I need you so badly! I want you right now more than I ever have! I'd kill myself if I thought this thing [killing her husband] would destroy us!"

Compare other new noir women, like Linda Farentino in John Dahl's 1994 film *The Last Seduction* and Theresa Russell again in *Black Widow*. These women take no prisoners. They will go on using their murderous wiles unless one day they are trapped by the law. What is interesting in 1980s new noir is that the male characters are more stupid and vulnerable than their 1940s predecessors. Compare William Hurt to Bill Pullman (who is murdered by Linda Farentino) and Nicol Williamson (who is poisoned by Theresa Russell). Sex and money are men's only objectives. All the males are sexually drawn to their mates, and the spider-women do them in. Women became more emancipated in the decade of the 1980s, and a neo-noir icon, like Kathleen Turner, who in the 1990s became a "lethal" protagonist, is the equal or better of any male counterpart.

When *Body Heat* was released in 1981, the film reviewers were extraordinarily kind. Everyone noted the similarity to Billy Wilder's 1944 noir classic, *Double Indemnity*; *Body Heat* capitalized on that parallel and succeeded on its own to gain an audience. As *Variety* rightly said, "[*Body Heat*] is an engrossing and mighty stylish meller (melodrama) in which sex and crime walk hand and hand down the path to tragedy. . . . [Kasdan] has brought the drama alive by steeping it in a humid, virtually oozing atmosphere. . . . In her film debut, Turner registers strongly as a hard gal with a past. Her deep-voiced delivery recalls that of a young Lauren Bacall" (another film noir icon of the 1940s). The *New York Times* agreed with *Variety*, as did most other newspapers and magazines, and even ran a special feature article on the "revival of film noir in the eighties." Clearly, *Body Heat* is a premier example of the new noir.

Body Heat was the first directorial effort for Lawrence Kasdan, who admittedly chose to revive the film noir style of the 1940s to ensure the success of his move from screenwriter to director. He is originally from Miami (the setting of *Body Heat*) and has gone on to other successful directorial efforts.

William Hurt is no stranger to neo-noir. He appeared in 1980 in a noir thriller entitled *Eyewitness*. However he prefers to tackle more complex roles, such as Valentin, the gay hairdresser in Hector Babenco's *Kiss of the Spider-woman*, for which he won the Best Actor Oscar of 1985.

In addition to the great work done by its leading actors, *Body Heat* contains some excellent performances by character actors Ted Danson, as a Fred Astaire–like dancing district attorney, and Mickey Rourke, in his debut role as a bomber who aids William Hurt in making murder seem like an accident. Rourke has became a new noir icon of sorts, starring in neo-noir films such as *Angel Heart* (1987) and *Johnny Handsome* (1989), a remake of Delmer Daves's celebrated noir classic, *Dark Passage* (1947).

One last comment about that fabulous music in *Body Heat*—it was composed by John Barry, who is known for many lush European and American film scores, among them *Out of Africa* and *Dances with Wolves*. Barry made his neo-noir scoring debut with *Body Heat* and later composed scores for *Hammett* (1982) and *Jagged Edge* (1984). He is best known internationally for his scoring of many James Bond films. His score for *Body Heat* is outstanding and ravishing, and it belongs in the canon of great noir and neo-noir film music. Barry's score punctuates the visuals with lyrical sensuality. And the Miranda Beach locale, adoringly photographed by Richard H. Kline, is viewed in all of its luxurious, languorous, and sultry beauty. The music also adds much flavor to the three very explicit sexual scenes between Hurt and Turner, especially one in a bathtub that leaves little to one's imagination. One decided advantage to the new noir then, is the revelation of sexuality as the protagonists' true motivation in committing crimes. Because of this tremendous relaxation of the production codes and the new film rating system, the neo-noir style is definitely here to stay.

12. BLOOD SIMPLE*** (1984)
97 minutes, Color

Director: Joel Coen.
Producer: Ethan Coen.
Screenplay: Joel Coen, Ethan Coen.
Photography: Barry Sonnenfeld.
Music: Carter Burwell.
Editing: Roderick Jaynes (Joel and Ethan Coen), Don Wiegmann.
Stars: John Getz, Frances McDormand, M. Emmet Walsh, Dan Hedaya.
DuArt Color. Circle Films. VHS & DVD: Circle Films.

Made on a low budget of $1.5 million, this is the Coen brothers' first film—a dandy of a neo-noir that uses the old formulas but reinvents them terrifically. It's the old, old story of a small-town Texas bar owner, Marty (played by Dan Hedaya), who hires a sleazy detective named Loren Visser (played by M. Emmet Walsh) to murder his wayward wife, Abby (Frances McDormand in her first film role) and her lover, Ray—one of Marty's bartenders (played by television actor John Getz). But where the shedding of blood is involved, there is nothing simple about it. The pleasure of this film is watching the characters trying to extricate themselves from a variety of plot twists.

In a simple film noir, the events leading to murder and mayhem would take place in linear fashion, usually leading to a predictable ending. In a Coen brothers' new noir, the chaos theory kicks in, and all plans spiral out of control in a series of double-crosses and brutal murders. Yes, Marty did hire Visser, first to spy on his adulterous wife and then to kill the unfaithful pair for the sum of ten thousand dollars. Taking a photo of the sleeping couple, Visser doctors it, making it look as if he had shot them both while sleeping—bullet holes and blood stains everywhere. He shows the phony photo to Marty and demands his ten thousand dollars. Marty retches in the bathroom and replaces the photo with an "Employees Must Wash Their Hands" sign, unknown to Visser. After Marty pays Visser, Visser shoots Marty dead, he thinks. Marty is seated at his desk in a chair, looking very dead, when Visser picks up his cash and the incriminating photo and leaves. At that point, Ray walks in to collect two weeks' pay owed to him and realizes Marty is dead, shot with the gun owned by Abby. Ray trundles Marty's body into his car and drives a considerable distance to some plowed fields, where he digs a grave for Marty. Sickened by the whole experience, Ray flees the car with the body in it. He returns only to find Marty is not in the car but alive, crawling out on the road. Ray retrieves him, places his body in a ditch, still alive, and buries him, whacking the sand with a shovel to keep him there.

Morning light comes up and Ray drives his car perpendicular to the furrows—a wonderful stylized shot. Anyone could tell where the body was buried if they looked carefully at the car tracks and the ditch. Ray is simply not too bright. Neither is Visser. When he realizes Marty switched the photo with a sign, he returns to the office to open the safe, but to no avail.

Meanwhile Ray has returned home, and Abby asks him what is going on between him and her husband. Ray tells her the story of Marty's burial, thinking Abby killed her husband and that his cover-up of the crime will cement their relationship. It only drives them further apart. This is emphasized when Ray is relating the story in his apartment: a newsboy offscreen hurtles a newspaper at the door—whomp!—and Abby is out of there.

Complications continue to confuse us. It seems Marty has been leaving messages on Ray's, Abby's, and Maurice's answering machines. Maurice goes to Ray's house, asking him why he took the safe from the office. (Maurice is a bartender played by Samm-Art Williams, an actor to watch in the future.) Ray knows nothing about it, and Abby returns to her home, that wide-windowed, unshaded apartment. There is another wonderful false and scary moment when Abby goes home and tries to sleep. She wakes up to see Marty sitting on her couch, ready to throttle her because of her infidelities. As Marty gets up, a huge quantity of blood spews from his mouth, and Abby suddenly wakes up in fear. Abby's dream is so real for us that we, the audience, begin to think Marty has come back from the grave.

The conclusion of *Blood Simple* is the real thrill of the film. Ray cannot eat or sleep after he buries Marty. He goes to Abby's apartment—we hear the huge ceiling fans making their monotonous "whump-whump"s. He believes he was followed by the man in the Volkswagen who had followed them during their first tryst. Ray also reveals he had found the safe, opened it, and found a photo of them, apparently dead with blood and bullet holes in their bodies. He urges Abby to turn off the lights. It is at that precise moment a rifle bullet blasts Ray through the back, killing him instantly. Abby believes it is Marty, back from the dead, seeking vengeance. Someone enters the apartment. We see it is Visser, first searching Ray's body for the missing photograph and then stalking Abby. The latter goes out the bathroom window into the adjoining room. Visser reaches through the window just as Abby stabs his right hand through with a knife, impaling the menacing private investigator, then working her way around the room to secure a gun and protect herself. Visser is in excruciating pain, screaming, firing bullets through the Sheetrock of the bathroom, sending rays of light through the bullet holes as he tries to kill Abby. (The last time I saw a director use this effect was in Fritz Lang's 1944 noir thriller, *Ministry of Fear*, in which Nazis fire through the door at the hero.)

Abby still believes it is Marty who is trying to kill her. She comes to the bathroom door just as Visser frees his right hand from the blade holding it, smashing his left one through the Sheetrock to do it. He takes a step toward opening the bathroom door. Abby shoots once, saying, "I'm not afraid of you, Marty!" Visser drops to the ground, mortally wounded. He replies, "I'll give him the message when I see him!" then expires. It is an ironic ending, as Abby does not know who she killed. The last view we have is of the underbelly of the bathroom sink, as Visser's eyes close to reveal blackness and the end title. A wonderful conclusion!

All the actors, especially Dan Hedaya and Frances McDormand, play their roles with such conviction—and M. Emmet Walsh is exceptionally good as the sexually leering, menacing Texas private eye. What makes this such an excellent new noir is that it is an artwork, totally conceived in a modern mode, not relying on rehashing the old formulas of Cain and Chandler and not derivative. Admittedly a grainy, underbudgeted film, a seedy tale of lust, murder, and revenge, *Blood Simple* is a tale of simple people in an ordinary town, placed under a great amount of pressure due to their adulterous natures, forced to work out their priorities and declare where their loyalties lie. It still amazes this viewer that the femme fatale (a scrubbed-faced McDormand) is the survivor of all the chaos around her and somewhat cynically believes she deserves to triumph. The Coen brothers' love of cinema shines through in the story line, the photography, the acting, and the editing. Their telling of this story of such a group of rotten people, unsympathetic lowlifes without any redeeming qualities, is sheer, delightful entertainment. And it is all totally believable in its new noir style!

13. TO LIVE AND DIE IN L.A.**** (1985)
116 minutes, Color

Director: William Friedkin.
Producer: Irving H. Levin.
Screenplay: William Friedkin, Gerald Petievich, based on Gerald Petievich's novel.
Photography: Robby Muller.
Music: Wayne Chung.
Editing: Bud S. Smith, M. Scott Smith.
Stars: William L. Peterson, Willem Dafoe, John Pankow, Debra Feuer, John Turturro.
Technicolor and Panavision. United Artists. VHS: Vestron for MGM/UA. DVD: MGM/UA.

Chaos, the operative factor in the Coen brothers' *Blood Simple*, reappears in William Friedkins's *To Live and Die in L.A.* The film has terrific visuals in Panavision by ace German cameraman Robbie Muller and a pulsating music score by Wayne Chung that literally melts into the visuals. This film tells the story of two FBI agents—William L. Peterson, as Richard Chance, and John Pankow, as John Vukovich—who take it upon themselves to bring to justice master counterfeiter Eric Masters (devastatingly played by Willem Dafoe).

The film begins with the murder of Thomas Bateman (Robert Downey Sr.), Peterson's partner. Following up a lead by himself, Bateman, according to Masters, "found himself in the wrong place at the wrong time"; Masters simply (and very brutally) blows Bateman away with his .44 Magnum, hiding his body in a dumpster. Bingo! Federal agents swoop in and discover the body, and Pankow is assigned as Peterson's new partner. Peterson vows he will bring in Dafoe at any cost, even if he has to violate the law. Peterson and Pankow go undercover and pretend to be buyers of counterfeit bills from Palm Springs. They even set up a deal with Dafoe but need thirty thousand dollars in front money. Dafoe realizes if the Palm Springs buyers are legitimate, they will be able to raise the cash (even if Peterson doesn't have a tan!). However, the FBI agent in charge of sting operations will give the partners only ten thousand dollars, the bureau's limit.

Through their informant Ruth Lanier (played beautifully by Darlanne Fluegel), the agents learn of an illegal "rough-diamond deal" going down in a few days; the Asian buyer is carrying fifty thousand dollars in cash. In desperation Peterson and Pankow waylay the courier and take the cash, only then realizing that the deal is an FBI sting operation; the Asian courier, whom they kill, is an FBI agent. They find themselves to be the villains. Moreover, in the third greatest car-chase scene ever made—after those in *Bullitt* (1968) and *The French Connection* (1971)—the agents escape detection *and* get away with the cash! The scenes in which they drive against traffic on the Los Angeles freeway are harrowing, completely believable, and caught beautifully by Robby Muller's camera.

In the final scenes of the film, Dafoe supplies the counterfeit bills to Peterson and Pankow, who then try to arrest him and his hulking Irish guard. Peterson is killed, a rifle blast directly in the face. Pankow lifts him up: "Speak to me, speak to me," and pursues the escaping Dafoe. The latter returns to his "factory" and incinerates all traces of evidence. Pankow finds him there, and Dafoe almost beats him to death with a heavy wooden beam. Pankow turns and fires on Dafoe, who is holding some combustible substance in his hand that sets the counterfeiter completely on fire, whirling around, screaming in an incendiary death. Justifiable and poetic! Pankow then returns to Petersons's informant's apartment. He insists she set Peterson up to get out from under his domain. Pankow demands that she work for him, or he will have her parole revoked. When he informs her of Peterson's death, she realizes she must cooperate in every way with Pankow (even sexually), or her life in Los Angeles will be over. Pankow, through all of these incidents, has changed dramatically— from square, honest, upright cop to savvy, realistic, and somewhat corrupt FBI agent.

The real beauties of this film are in the nuances of the performances. William L. Peterson is wonderfully athletic—he does bungee jumping off a Los Angeles bridge, "flying free until your balls come through your throat when you hit bottom." He is loyal to his ex-partner and wants to avenge his death, whatever the cost (even if it means risking his own life). He plays Darlanne Fleugel's lover, too. The film is extraordinarily frank in its nude love scenes, showing genitalia of both sexes at a respectable distance. Peterson's only physical fault is his bowleggedness—but he comes off as a dashing FBI agent, very macho in jeans and cowboy boots, nevertheless. The last frame of the film, after the entire roll up of the end titles, shows him as a young stud, a romantic icon who has given his life to do a good job.

On the other hand, Willem Dafoe as Eric Masters practically steals the film from every actor, male or female. His hairless, white, physically slender body is often seen in the nude, especially with his bisexual girlfriend. Dafoe's character is all action and playfulness, simmering charm and danger. He strives for perfection as a counterfeiter and artist. In fact, Friedkin's opening scene shows Dafoe making hundreds of identical twenty-dollar bills. When Dafoe is displeased with a canvas he has painted, he sets it on fire after carefully attaching it to a wall. (The figure in the painting had eyes like his and perhaps prefigures his own death by fire.) If Dafoe is having sex with his girlfriend, Bianca (played by Debra Feuer), he videotapes the entire experience and uses monitors so that they can watch themselves copulating as a further sexual turn-on. On one occasion, he gives his girl-friend a present—a female whore clad in sexy underclothes is a plaything for the evening. Dafoe lives for danger, always on the edge, and dies an excruciatingly painful death by fire at the conclusion. There could be no other destiny but that one for him.

Dean Stockwell also gives a brilliant, understated performance as an attorney for the mob. He is Dafoe's legal contact and advises Pankow about his rights after the killing of the Asian FBI agent, "but he cannot get directly involved."

Dafoe's girlfriend is his sexual equal and almost his partner in crime in the counterfeiting scheme. She is also a ballet dancer, and we watch parts of two performances in the film. Dafoe's lust for her is obvious, as he takes down her costume and begins to fondle her nipples orally in view of other women in the dance company but out of the camera's view. When Dafoe dies, she goes off in Dafoe's black racing car and continues living her bisexual, dangerous, criminal life.

Friedkin's film is so definitely new noir—the outrageous pulsating musical score combined with the open sexual ferocity between men and women (and women and women) on both sides of the law is refreshingly on target for a mid-1980s movie audience. Freidkin also excels in the use of helicopter shots and second unit photography, which show to fine effect his car chases, as well as periodic assaults on various criminals.

Character actor John Turturro also shows up in the film as a courier for Dafoe, caught and imprisoned by the FBI; he later gets away from Peterson and is apprehended again by the latter. His street language is vile, totally believable. He is almost killed in a subplot; Dafoe believes he is going to "spill the beans about his entire operation" and tries unsuccessfully to have him killed in prison by two black hoods.

There is a lot of machismo attitude going down in *To Live and Die in L.A.*—machismo between blacks, on the take for drugs and counterfeit bills, and whites, the creators and passers of the bills for illegal profits—both sides wanting to set the record straight. For example, when Max Waxman (played by Christopher Allport) steals six hundred thousand dollars from Dafoe, the latter uses his girlfriend to entice Waxman sexually so he can enter the house to get the drop on Waxman and recover his cash. Waxman opens the safe and tries to kill Dafoe with a hidden gun; Dafoe kills him, in full view of an FBI stakeout across the street, with Pankow sleeping at his post. It seems the criminals are more feisty than the FBI agents, who are sometimes sleeping on the job.

What makes *To Live and Die in L.A.* so fascinating is the good cop/bad cop element—Pankow versus Peterson. Both men are flawed, vulnerable characters. They make terrible mistakes and they pay for them (the death of Robert Downey Sr., Peterson's first partner). The villains, too, are attractive, glamorous, but they are flawed characters and meet predictable and extraordinary fates. Villains and good guys both share extraordinarily cynical attitudes. Peterson and Pankow are two raw recruits, cynical FBI agents on the trail of a smart, shrewd counterfeiter—Dafoe at his most slithering, snakelike best. All of them are salivating over the cash they rip off (legally or illegally) or spend in the most exhilarating manner. But Friedkin manages to keep the story contained on a "Dirty Harry" level, having Peterson act as a federal agent willing to rob, kill, and exploit everyone in his path to track down and bring to justice the killer of his partner. What is new here is that Peterson is willing to bring his new partner (Pankow) and his paroled-informant girlfriend (Fleugel) down with him.

The ballsy script has some excellent crook-on-crook and crook-on-cop dialogue taken from real life. Written by a former Secret Service agent, Gerald Petievich, *To Live and Die in L.A.* is especially good because Friedkin uses a cast of virtually unknown performers and gives each of their roles a sexual charge. In addition, this new noir features some homoerotic scenes and unusually explicit male nudity, which had not been seen on American screens before. Robby Muller's glorious photography captures the merging of new villainous roles in attractive settings, and Wayne Chung's score perfectly melds with the fabulous settings. We sympathize with both heroes and villains and never have time to search for the meaning, correctness, or consequences of their actions.

To Live and Die in L.A. remains a hyperventilatingly intense film—extremely violent, one of the new noirs that have plenty of action and passion for both good guys and criminals. Most 1980s critics misunderstood this film because it violates the rules of film noir. It tends to obfuscate the line between good and bad guys, and in doing so, presents us with an ambiguous universe. Both good and bad guys have to die in order to be made sympathetic to us, and both make mistakes that they pay for—a quality new to 1980s crime films. *To Live and Die in L.A.* is perhaps the most flagrant example of this new kind of noir, with its extremely stylized photography, sets, music, and screenplay. These elements mesh perfectly with contemporary Los Angeles and all of the actors' performances. It is a thrilling, unpredictable, totally energetic film that takes you on a two-hour ride to its startling, unpredictable conclusion. This is probably director William Friedkin's best film ever and his best contribution to the new noir style.

14. AT CLOSE RANGE**** (1986)
111 minutes, Color

Director: James Foley.
Producers: Don Guest, Elliott Lewis.
Screenplay: Nicholas Kazan.
Photography: Juan Ruiz-Anchia.
Music: Patrick Leonard.
Editing: Donn Aron, Howard E. Smith.
Stars: Sean Penn, Christopher Walken, Mary Stuart Masterson, Chris Penn.
Color by CFI. Orion Pictures. VHS & DVD: Vestron.

By the mid-1980s, the new noir style had begun to turn its attention to less spectacular subjects than crime films with unique car chases (*French Connection*) or reprises of film noir plots (*Blood Simple*). It had begun to focus attention on some true stories. Singular family-problem films with dark facets were filmed in bucolic areas; in these films dark characters with dark moods and dark deeds are found quite unexpectedly, revealed through lyrical slow motion photography and poetic photographic effects in bright sunlight.

Such is *At Close Range*, a James Foley film shot in sunny, natural landscapes and based on true incidents. In the film, a murderous rural Pennsylvania family of thieves—people of whom you would least expect it—commit barbarous acts against other people and one another with unmitigated evil intent.

Based on a story by Nicholas Kazan, *At Close Range* is about a real small-time hood and leader of a local crime ring (menacingly played by Christopher Walken in one of his best roles). The film begins very slowly, almost poetically. We first see Sean Penn as Brad Whitewood Jr. driving his pickup truck into the local town and around the town square. It's a hot Saturday night and blond Brad is looking for companionship. He spies townie Terry (played by Mary Stuart Masterson), a sixteen-year-old girl who has a date with a girlfriend. After some polite conversation about how much he likes her smile, they arrange to meet in the same place two evenings later. Next, Sean picks up his brother Christopher Penn (a real casting coup), who plays Tommy Whitewood, his half brother. Both are restless teenagers, popping pills, looking for girls and booze. Not finding any action, they drive home to the house of their remarried mother (Julie Whitewood, played by *Diary of Anne Frank* star Millie Perkins). Her itinerant ex-husband, Brad Whitewood Sr. (Walken) suddenly returns home for a visit. He has in tow a "family" of criminals. Among the more interesting of them is David Strathairn as a drug addict named Tony Pine One, an old-time con artist called Patch (played by Tracey Walter), and Candy Clark as Mary Sue, Walken's new mistress.

Walken returns a hail-fellow-well-met by his sons, but they realize something is off center about their father—especially his reputation. Brad Jr. never got out of high school and can't hold down a job; he has become a petty thief but has not committed any major crimes, as yet. But he is easily lured into his father's band of professional thieves and enjoys the early rewards of his new career. His affair has begun with Terry; she convinces Brad Jr. to join the gang and insists on his participation in front of a meeting of the entire group. To prove he has the guts to enter the professional group, with his teenage gang, Brad pulls a few heists. Among the participants are Crispin Glover as Lucas and Kiefer Sutherland as Tim. Stealing tractors and farm equipment comes easily, and Brad Jr. and his group are quite successful at it. Brad is accepted by his father into the "family." "We're blood!" Walken screams, and everything seems fine until, one evening, Brad Sr. orders the drowning of a police informant named Lester (Jake Dengel). Brad Jr. watches, and Walken puts his fingers to his lips, signaling, "Don't tell!"

Brad Jr. is ultimately horrified by the kind of person he has become and also upset at his new responsibilities to his father. When he tries to extricate himself from his father's gang and strike out on his own, he is caught by police during his first heist of farm equipment and tractors. Brad is the only one of his group held in jail, and on extremely high bail; the cops want Brad Jr. to inform on his dad, the ultimate culprit. When Brad Sr. rapes Terry after getting her drunk, Terry realizes she has to get Brad Jr. to leave Pennsylvania for her brother's farm in Montana.

There is a wonderful scene in which Christopher Walken absolutely snaps, worried that Brad Jr. might give away his entire operation and the identity of his "family." Walken drives his red pickup truck into a field, circling and circling around, dust flying everywhere, until he eventually stops and realizes what course of action he must take. Brad Sr. kills off all the members of Brad Jr.'s teenage gang, walking them to their own graves, and kills his own son—Brad Jr.'s brother, Tommy. Penn is pushed over the edge and realizes what a dysfunctional family he has. Before Brad Sr. kills Tommy, he asks him, "Will you tell the grand jury anything?" Tommy answers, "Of course not, Dad." Walken shouts, "Liar!" and pulls the trigger, whose sound is heard echoing into the next scene.

Of course Walken has the outstanding role as the charismatic criminal, ostensibly successful at grand scale robbery. He is a kind of Pennsylvania *padrino* (godfather), leading a small army of goons to do his dirty work. Walken is both charming and lethal, sensual and cruel—a father without a heart, willing to kill his own sons to survive—so totally *evil*.

Sean Penn as Brad Jr. builds his performance slowly. First he is a pitiful teenager and inept thief; then through love, he recognizes the truth about his minuscule life, his father, and their dysfunctional family life.

Although *At Close Range* displays some of the psychotic interior notions of film noir, its heightened rustic visuals, its often stunning external landscapes, liberate it and place it in new noir territory. The rustic, referential imagery calls the viewer's attention away from the plot itself to the director's self-conscious effort to create deeper resonance: empty fields in which vans await stolen merchandise, darkened banks along moonlit flowing rivers where drownings take place to silence informers, green hillsides where graves are already dug for intended victims.

At Close Range is an idiosyncratic film whose new noir style tells you the story is about more than small-time hoods in rural Pennsylvania. Brad Sr.'s kind of evil is beyond words—even his Pennsylvania rural accent distorts what he is saying. Brad Jr. discusses how much he is like his father—all seething rage, he knows he is trapped by his father's spirit. It is his love for the sixteen-year-old Terry that liberates him from seeking his father's love and from the nothingness of the life he lives with his mother and abusive stepfather. At first, he wants to join his father's gang and live with Terry "outside of the law"; he tries to prove his equality and manhood to his father through his "kiddie-gang heists." But when the gang heists go awry, it is too late for Brad to escape his father's grip. Brad Jr. is arrested when he tries to get the money to escape with Terry. Brad Sr. rapes Terry as a warning to his son about what happens to informers, and Brad Jr., who has already witnessed the murder of the informant Lester, comes clean to the authorities in exchange for his release from custody. Finally, Brad Sr. gives orders for his own son's murder as he salaciously watches a stripper in a local Pennsylvania bar, noting the time on his watch. As Brad Jr. and Terry leave in his car for Montana, multiple gunshots ring out—Terry is killed and Brad is badly wounded but survives. He goes to his father's house, finds the "family gun," and, losing blood, holds Brad Sr. at bay, wanting him " to die one day at a time" in jail.

The screen goes white and we are at a courthouse in some large Pennsylvania city. Helicopters fly in father and son, and Brad Jr. is asked his relationship to the accused. In a muffled and tearful voice, he utters ashamedly, "He's my father!" End title.

It is interesting to note that Terry (Mary Stuart Masterson) is the catalyst for the battle between father and son. Although Brad Jr. is the initial pursuer of this seemingly virtuous town girl, she is quick to reject her background and encourages Brad Jr.'s alliance with his father. She flirts with the evil father, who eventually rapes her as a means of self-protection and insuring his own paternal power. It is Terry who helps lure Brad Jr. into criminality (as would a temptress of old) and causes the inescapable confrontation with his father. At one point, Brad Jr. says to his father, "I knew I loved Terry, but when she died, I knew I had to come back and take care of you."

The new noir style, as executed by director James Foley, opens up the story's material to display many darkly resonant themes—the power of good over evil, the sins of the father visited on the son, and the search for the lost father and the ultimate desire for atonement. Foley closely interconnects his vision of the story and the adolescent world of his antihero/outlaw/noir character and then develops the mythic themes of Brad Jr.'s search for his departed father. But ultimately, when Brad Jr. witnesses the murder of Lester, the informant, and Brad Sr. puts his fingers to his lips—signaling silence and complicity—Brad Jr. realizes his father is truly evil and capable of anything. That is why he must turn him over to the law. Brad Jr. retrieves the "family gun" from a bathroom shelf and says to his father, "Is this the gun that killed everyone dear to me?" He begins to fire away, and we wonder, when the screen goes white, whether Brad Jr. passed out and the father triumphed. The courthouse ending feels tacked on, and in this era, when crime does pay, perhaps it is somewhat theatrical. However, Penn and Walken give the performances of their lives in this wonderful new noir that has been underrated totally by most film critics. *At Close Range* certainly boosted Sean Penn's career. He went on to a full-bodied career as a neo-noir hero: in the excellent 1990 Phil Joanou film *State of Grace* he played an Irish undercover cop, and some years later he played a Boston gangster in Clint Eastwood's dark film *Mystic River* (2003).

At Close Range also has an excellent music score by composer Patrick Leonard that resonates with the visuals of Spanish cinematographer Juan Ruiz-Anchia. What is especially interesting is the lighting of the interiors of some of the rural houses and restaurants. Swaths of afternoon sunlight come through open windows as some of the characters, sitting in shadows, discuss their fates or their plans for future victims. These scenes are very painterly, recalling the great Goya paintings in which swatches of sunlight illuminate parts of a room *and* you can almost see the dust rising from the floor sparkling in the air. *At Close Range* has a wonderful photographic artfulness and should be commended for it. One hopes more Spanish cinematographers with the talent of Ruiz-Anchia find their way into the American film industry. Amazing artful photography is one of the new stylistic features of neo-noir.

15. FATAL ATTRACTION*** (1987)
119 minutes, Color

Director: Adrian Lyne.
Producer: Stanley R. Jaffe, Sherry Lansing.
Screenplay: James Dearden (based on his original 1979 screenplay *Diversion*), Nicholas Meyer.
Photography: Howard Atherton.
Music: Maurice Jarre.
Editing: Peter E. Berger, Michael Kahn.
Stars: Michael Douglas, Glenn Close, Anne Archer.
Technicolor. Paramount. VHS & DVD: Paramount. [Also released in a director's cut version with an alternate ending.]

Femmes fatales have always been successful seducing their victims and using them for their own purposes. In *Fatal Attraction*, Glenn Close plays a femme fatale named Alex Forrest, an associate editor for a New York publishing firm who meets lawyer Dan Gallagher (played by Michael Douglas) at a press party that the latter is attending with his wife, Beth (played by Anne Archer.) Alex and Dan meet once again at a weekend office meeting when Dan's wife and young daughter are out of town, visiting the wife's parents in Mount Kisco and house hunting. The sexual attraction is certainly there, and Alex lures Dan to her Soho loft, where they are so hot sexually, they tear off their clothes and begin to make love in her kitchen sink. With the new kind of noir film, there is a greater freedom in showing male and female nudity, especially women's exposed breasts and erect nipples. What we believe is just a one-night stand between two consenting mature adults certainly hops the track plotwise. For in the new noir, Alex becomes a "killer" femme fatale who wants to continue the affair, claiming she is pregnant and wanting Dan to share her life even though he has a wife and child of his own and has a truly happy marriage.

The new noir, besides showing explosively erotic sex scenes, demonstrates a penchant for psychotic women who become involved in revenge fantasies if they do not have their way. Following Congreve's dictum, "Heaven has no rage, like love to hatred turned, nor Hell a fury like a woman scorned," director Adrian Lyne pulls no punches in showing the virago Alex Forrester becomes and how she tries to win Dan back after their evenings together. The film operates on the premise that there is no safe sex. Dan watches his future as a law partner in an established Manhattan firm almost go down the drain, along with his marriage, as the deranged Alex (played by Glenn

Close) first tosses acid on his car, destroying it completely, then kills his daughter's pet rabbit, boiling it to death on the stove of his new country house. Alex's sexual paranoia runs rampant, and she comes on to Dan as he tries to throttle her in her Soho apartment, but realizes he is a good, ethical person and cannot kill.

The filmmakers establish Alex as a career woman—she is thirty-six years old, single, and given to having transient affairs. She has missed her chance at love, security, and happiness with a husband and children, and we see her as lonely, somewhat demented, and clearly giving us the downside of a supposedly liberated woman's life. The new noir woman is given to pathological problems, and in *Fatal Attraction* she becomes a knife-wielding psychopath. She is given to moods of morose behavior. For instance, she sits alone listening to the opera *Madame Butterfly*, absentmindedly turning her living room lamp on and off, while a pair of tickets to the Metropolitan Opera production sit unused on a counter after her one-night stand. Having already tried suicide by slitting her wrists after her first evening with Dan, she compliments him for his fortitude in staying with her and later says she should not have put him through all of her paranoia. The kitchen knife reappears as a weapon in the final scene of the film: Alex has entered the bathroom of the Gallagher's country house while Beth, Dan's wife, is preparing a bath. Dan has already told his wife the truth about his one-night stand with Alex. When Beth clears the moisture-laden bathroom mirror with the sleeve of her robe, she sees Alex standing there with the butcher knife, about to dispatch her.

Almost like an Alfred Hitchcock film noir suspense thriller, *Fatal Attraction* becomes a new noir thriller with an over-the-top ending. Alex has done so much to Dan and his family (the final straw is the afternoon kidnapping of his daughter—returned unharmed after Alex takes her on a roller coaster ride—which causes worried Beth to drive carelessly into a car accident) that if Alex were killed, it would certainly be understood by the Mount Kisco police.

Returning to the final scene in the bathroom and Alex's threats to kill Beth, for the first time we witness her dementia—she even cuts herself on her left thigh as she talks crazily (and somewhat dazedly) about how Beth is destroying her life with Dan and their future child. The whistle is blowing on the tea kettle in the kitchen, and Dan removes it from the stove; he then hears Beth screaming and races up the stairs. It seems to take him an eternity, but he goes through the door just as Alex is about to plunge her huge butcher knife into Beth's body, lying on the floor. Alex slashes at Dan, who finally grabs her around the neck and forces her head under the water of the overflowing bathtub. He holds her down fiercely until there are no bubbles issuing from her mouth, her eyes wide open but not seeing. Dan turns, about to caress his wife, but Alex suddenly rises up with a banshee scream, wielding the knife at Dan. At that point, Beth comes through the door with a gun and shoots Alex once in the torso, and the latter expires for certain, her body sliding down the wall into the bathtub, her eyes closed and head, turned toward the wall, sinking into the water. The police arrive, and the camera wanders over photographs of Dan, his wife, and their daughter during happier times.

We must note also how protective Beth is of her husband and her family. When Dan first reveals his affair with Alex to his wife, Beth says to Alex on the telephone, "If you bother me or my family again, I will kill you!" Obviously hurt by Dan's affair, she throws her husband out of the house. But after her auto accident she recognizes her true love for him, despite his transgression, and takes him back. Beth also finds the strength, both moral and physical, to dispatch Alex with her family gun. Obviously, the family that *kills* together, stays together. And we have sympathy for the entire family, especially given all of the ordeals they have been put through.

Interestingly enough, the alternate ending, which was shown theatrically in Japan and on French television, has Alex committing suicide with the butcher knife; but it has Dan's fingerprints on it, making him responsible for her "murder"! Glenn Close's performance is so suffocating, convincing, darkly deranged, and profoundly unsympathetic that the producers felt her being killed by Anne Archer was the proper way to end the film. In fact, Archer is so good as Beth—a woman who is beautiful, self-assured, sexy, aware of the world around her, fulfilled, a successful wife and mother—that she can serve as the instrument of Alex's demise and be applauded for it. If the Michael Douglas character had had some darker noir-like atmosphere about him—Dan as betrayer/user of women, irresponsible—then perhaps the suicide/revenge ending might have worked. But Douglas plays the role straight, as a good guy, kind of average, even goofy in a very complacent, unexciting way, and we are convinced by his attempts to do the decent thing— something the paranoid and demented Alex could never understand. *Fatal Attraction* gives away its conclusion in the title, but offers a useful message: it's great to be sexy and have a good time, but the cost may be high, especially in an extramarital relationship.

16. THE GRIFTERS**** (1990)
114 minutes, Color

Director: Stephen Frears.
Producers: Robert Harris, Jim Painter, Martin Scorsese.
Screenplay: Donald E. Westlake, based on Jim Thompson's novel.
Photography: Oliver Stapleton.
Music: Elmer Bernstein.
Editing: Mick Audsley.
Stars: Anjelica Huston, John Cusack, Annette Bening.
Technicolor and Panavision. Miramax. VHS & DVD: Miramax.

> I wined and dined on mulligan stew and never wished for turkey,
> As I hitched and hiked and *grifted* too from Maine to Albuquerque.
>
> —Lorenz Hart and Richard Rodgers, "The Lady Is a Tramp"

The Grifters is probably the toughest of the new noirs to be filmed at the beginning of the 1990s. Based on an equally tough novel by Jim Thompson, whose body of work has been recently discovered by new producers and directors (*The Kill-Off; The Hot Spot; After Dark, My Sweet; This World, Then the Fireworks* among others), *The Grifters* is one of the new noirs to use the old noir stylistics and combine them with the newest technologies. Because of the relaxation of censorship codes, the film leaves an indelibly frank and outrageous mark on its viewers; it is leavened with cynicism, hard irony, and even a sense of humor.

The titles are placed against a background of black-and-white 1950s photos of Los Angeles, until a 1950s two-door Cadillac appears in motion and the screen suddenly turns to Technicolor. Anjelica Huston as Lilly Dillon is driving to the Paloma Downs racetrack as Martin Scorsese, the film's producer, in a voice-over tells us that Lilly works for a Baltimore-based gambling organization that changes the odds on horses, grifting the track and keeping the odds in their favor so as not to pay out huge sums of money to bettors. Then director Stephen Frears does something very unusual. He uses a split screen to show Lilly working as her son, Roy Dillon (played by John Cusack), occupies a second frame, fleecing a bartender out of change for a twenty-dollar bill by giving him a ten-dollar bill instead. Then Annette Bening, as Myra Langtry, moves onscreen, making it a triptych; she tries to fleece a jewelry store owner out of cash, claiming she has a real diamond bracelet to sell when it is actually glass. All three are wearing dark glasses, their trademark as grifters, and are caught simultaneously facing the camera.

Then the camera follows only Roy, and the clever triptych is reduced to only one story on the Panavision screen.

Roy is a grifter on the small con, in for the small take. We see him going into another bar, pulling the same stunt—flashing the twenty-dollar bill and giving the bartender a ten-dollar bill after he has made change for the twenty—but this time, the bartender is wise to the con, and with a baseball bat, he severely wounds Roy in the stomach. Roy retreats home, to a dismal apartment/hotel in downtown Los Angeles, where Myra also lives. Myra arrives in Roy's apartment, where we learn they have had an ongoing affair. Roy grabs at Myra's breasts playfully, calling them the "twins" and saying he wants to take them to bed, but he feels ill. What Roy does not know is that Myra is looking for a partner—a player of the big con, for which she acted as a ringer, bringing men with money to Cole Langly (J. T. Walsh in one of his best roles as a con man) to fleece them out of their cash.

There are two elaborate dream sequences or flashbacks in the film. The first occurs in Roy's apartment as he is tuning in and out of consciousness. He is seventeen, on his own, and he meets a grifter. Roy asks him to show him all the tricks, because Roy has no real job and wants to make his living on the grift. The second flashback takes place in La Jolla, when Myra relates to Roy everything about the big con: she and Cole stole a Texas oilman's money, Cole pretending to go mad and shoot Myra dead in his office as the Texan flees—"After that, they never come back." Unfortunately, Cole was a prisoner of stress and is now in Tascadero, a state mental institution. Myra propositions Roy, who will not participate, even with the old lure of sex.

Previous to this last scene, Roy's mother, Lilly, visits him on the way to a racetrack. She finds Roy is ill, calls a doctor "for the mob" who puts Roy in the hospital; he is apparently hemorrhaging from the baseball-bat incident. Roy survives, and Myra starts asking questions about Lilly's past life and work. Roy does not tell her anything, but Myra begins to follow Lilly's Cadillac and, with binoculars, notices the stash of money that Lilly keeps in her trunk. Since Myra is mob connected she calls Baltimore and tells Bobo Justus, Lilly's boss and mentor, about Lilly's stash. Lilly is forced into hiding when she is tipped by the mob that Bobo is after her.

There is an earlier scene in which Bobo (dramatically played by Pat Hingle) checks up on Lilly's work because she didn't succeed in lowering the odds on certain bets. Lilly tells the truth about her son and his illness. Nevertheless, Bobo brutally hits her in the stomach with his fist and threatens her with several oranges wrapped in a towel; the oranges will not cause bruises, but, if used correctly, could damage her insides. We are led to believe Bobo will punish Lilly in this manner, but instead he lets the towel go, and with a huge well-lit cigar, he burns a hole on top of her right hand. Lilly therefore has good cause to worry about Bobo and the mob, especially when she finds out Myra told them about her stash. Myra did this so she could obtain Lilly's money to participate in another big con, with or without Roy. Lilly escapes the mob and drives to Phoenix with Myra following her. Myra sneaks into Lilly's motel room and tries to choke her to death, but Lilly kills Myra with a blast from her silencer into her mouth. Roy is called to Phoenix to identify his mother's body. He picks up her right hand—no cigar burn—and realizes it is Myra who is dead. When Roy returns to his Los Angeles apartment, he finds Lilly there dressed in Myra's clothes. She has found Roy's stash of money hidden behind two paintings of clowns and demands it from Roy. Roy says he is off the short con but needs the money. Lilly will do anything to survive.

The last scene is as thrilling as it is believable. Lilly comes on to Roy sexually—she will do anything for the money! (Myra suspected Roy had a thing for his mother but didn't even realize it, and Roy throws Myra out for her disgusting insinuation.) We have come full circle. Just as Roy veers away from Lilly, she hits him with the attaché case holding the money. The glass of water Roy is holding shatters, leaving a huge shard in Roy's jugular. Roy bleeds to death. Sobbing, Lilly nevertheless gathers up all the money, takes Roy's car, and drives into the night. End title.

The Grifters is one of the best of the new noirs ever made. All the actors—Anjelica Huston, John Cusack, and Annette Bening—excel in their roles. The film is a dark noir with a terrific script and dialogue by crime writer Donald Westlake. The film really moves—the action is brisk, amoral; the motivations are sleazy and cynical. Cusack tries to retain his bland anonymity but falls into deep trouble. Huston is dangerous to both her son and his lover, Myra. In fact, the women have some of the best, bitchiest lines in the film, carping about age, motherhood, and morality. Bening gives one of the two best performances of her life (the other was in *American Beauty* [1999]) as the feline Myra—she's pure cat. She slithers through the film with her clothes on and off, taking sexual manipulation to a new level. Pat Hingle, usually the good guy in films, has his heaviest role and commits acts of pure cruelty. Most important, the film is really a study of the three principal lead characters and does not fall into the mire of a plot machine. The director, Stephen Frears, who began his career in England in the 1980s with *My Beautiful Laundrette*, has captured the truly American mean-spiritedness and cynicism of the Jim Thompson novel, exposing the gritty underbelly of the con game, and given it an existential bite without any moral center in 1950s Los Angeles. The film is especially slinky and low when we realize that all these people do is con people out of money any which way they can—there is no real love or trust—and everyone is vulnerable.

One last note: without Elmer Bernstein's wonderful, moody noir score, this film could have been much less successful. As it stands, Bernstein's score accentuates the ice-cold, tough, hard-as-nails, gripping atmosphere in a lush Los Angeles, full of color but with no real heart.

17. RESERVOIR DOGS**** (1992)
105 minutes, Color

Director: Quentin Tarantino.
Producer: Lawrence Bender.
Screenplay: Quentin Tarantino.
Photography: Andrzej Sekula.
Music Supervisor: Karyn Rachtman.
Editing: Sally Menke.
Stars: Harvey Keitel, Tim Roth, Michael Madsen, Steve Buscemi, Chris Penn, Lawrence Tierney, Quentin Tarantino.
Eastmancolor and Panavision. Miramax. VHS & DVD: Miramax.

When John Garfield utters the immortal words at the end of Robert Rossen's *Body and Soul* (1947)—"Everybody dies!"—he challenges the boxing mob and also gives the leitmotif for Quentin Tarantino's debut film, *Reservoir Dogs.* "Everybody dies, almost." Messrs. Orange, White, Brown, Blue, Yellow, and Blonde receive their just desserts, as do their gang leader, Joe Cabot (played by octogenarian Lawrence Tierney), and his son Eddie (played by a corpulent Christopher Penn). All of the men with color-coded names are killed during and after a diamond heist that goes awry, as well as the gang leader and his son. Lawrence Tierney is a real film noir icon; he established himself in the mid-1940s in *Dillinger*, a Monogram film, and in the late 1940s and early 1950s played tough-guy roles in *Born to Kill* and *The Hoodlum.* When he worked for RKO Radio Pictures, he was the only character actor who had true evil in his eyes. Tarantino certainly made a casting coup when he put Tierney in the role of gang leader.

As the film opens, the group assembled for breakfast consists of all new noir actors. Quentin Tarantino, a former videostore employee, certainly knows how to walk the walk and talk the talk. He specializes in keen, acerbic, and trendy dialogue sprinkled with racist jargon and sexual pejoratives, as well as in time refractions (flashbacks and flash-forwards). We first meet this group of hold-up men early in the morning at a Los Angeles joint, where their meal is hosted by Joe Cabot. Their conversation is macho and trivial, as they discuss Madonna's song "Like a Virgin" and the practice of "tipping." All agree to participate in the heist, which the audience never sees—the heist of a diamond merchandiser whose firm has already been staked out by the police because of information provided by one of the gang. Tim Roth is Mr. Orange, who operates as an undercover cop and has infiltrated the mob.

Roth and Mr. White (Harvey Keitel) commandeer a woman's car in their attempt to flee the crime scene. Roth is shot in the stomach and begins slowly bleeding to death. He kills an innocent woman, afraid to blow his cover, and is helped by Mr. White to retreat to a local warehouse where every gang member will rendezvous to split the profits of the theft.

At the warehouse, White and Orange are the first to arrive. Orange is bleeding profusely, and White does his best to comfort him. Mr. Pink (Steve Buscemi) shows up next, carrying a satchel full of diamonds. They all are waiting for the big boss, Joe Cabot (Tierney), and the rest of the gang to arrive. Mr. Blonde (chillingly played by Michael Madsen) enters and later brings in a cop he captured and threw in the trunk of his car. The cop is lashed down to a chair with duct tape; everyone there agrees there is an informant, and the captured cop might know his identity. In the most devastating torture scene I have ever seen in a film, Mr. Blonde dances to a song called "Stuck in the Middle with You" with a switchblade razor in his right hand; the camera moves left, focusing on an empty hall-way when we hear the blood-curdling screams of the helpless policeman, whose mouth is bound with silver duct tape. Mr. Blonde walks into cam-era range, holding the cop's bloody right ear. It is such a visceral scene, and the only time I ever rose out of my seat and shouted in a Manhattan theater was when I saw it. The theater was filled with stunned faces: "Oh God, no."

Tarantino uses flash-forwards and flashbacks to refract linear time: we are suddenly present at the scene of the crime in its aftermath, watching the gang flee. We are also present at two preparation meetings before the actual robbery, as well as at Mr. Orange's meeting with a black undercover cop. The cop urges Mr. Orange to act out a four-page prepared story in which the cop successfully avoids being busted by Los Angeles cops while carrying drugs in a bathroom with narcs and a sniffing police dog present. *Reservoir Dogs* has much in the way of low language, racist stereotyping, machismo attitudes, and cynical humor.

The conclusion is the best part of the film. Mr. Orange kills Mr. Blonde after the latter empties a whole can of gasoline on the cop to immolate him. Orange empties his entire cartridge of shells into Mr. Blonde for the sadistic way he tortured the captured cop. Orange now has no choice but to reveal his true identity to the bound and mutilated victim seated in the chair. At this point, Christopher Penn (Tierney's son Eddie) arrives, sees the cop tied to the chair, and ruthlessly pumps three bullets into him. Ed-die may have believed the cop was working with the informant. Joe Cabot arrives on the scene. When he threatens to kill Mr. Orange, Mr. White warns him not to do it. Cabot is convinced Mr. Orange is the informant— "I didn't check him out 100 percent, the only one." The four of them raise their guns to each other, threatening, talking. Nobody backs down. They all shoot simultaneously in a free-for-all and kill one another instantly. Mr. Pink (Steve Buscemi), seeing the carnage, picks up the satchel loaded with diamonds and leaves through the front door. He was washing his hands when all this occurred—the least likely survivor to leave the warehouse alive with the big boodle. Keitel survives for a few minutes, cradling Roth in his arms when Roth admits the truth about his complicity with the law. Cops arrive and Keitel dies in a shoot-out with them.

Reservoir Dogs (there must be some significance to the title) is a straight, tough-as-nails, new noir crime film owing much to Stanley Kubrick's 1956 heist film *The Killing*—although Tarantino prefers to show not the heist but the consequences of it. The rules are no longer "Crime doesn't pay" and "Bad guys don't get away with murder" but "Crime does pay" and "Bad guys suffer terrible ends." Tarantino chose all of his actors wisely, especially Lawrence Tierney, linking 1940s noir to 1990s new noir. English actor Tim Roth is especially good as Mr. Orange, assimilating an American accent. Harvey Keitel always gives a credible performance as a hood, since he grew up in Brooklyn with men of this ilk. Michael Madsen adds a lyrical note to his role, dancing and cavorting while doing his evil and unforgettable torture scene. Crooked-toothed Steve Buscemi gives one of his irascible performances as a hood with a sense of humor. Christopher Penn, who gained an enormous amount of weight between making *At Close Range* and this film, physically gives a strong, no-nonsense performance as the son of mob boss Tierney, shooting first and asking questions later. Penn's last speech, defying Orange's assertion that Mr. Blonde is the informant, is graphic and startlingly convincing.

We get to know very little about the other side of the law, the cops. We're given glimpses at the lives of some undercover cops and narcs who patrol bathrooms, but the film concentrates mainly on the lives and deaths of the thieves. Tarantino was especially wise to concentrate only on the major actors, who carry the story through to its breathtaking and fiendish conclusion. Abetted by source music that plays on a radio station featuring "K. Billy's Super Sounds of the 1970s," the silences of the film loom large. They are charged with a gritty reality and criminality that give the film a cold, wet darkness (despite California daylight and color) that stays with us long after the film ends. This new noir film is intelligent and visceral at the same time, a riveting experience. Although the film looks like a low-budget entry in the B-movie category, it has excellent A-movie performances all the way—and it was wise for the director, in his cameo role of Mr. Brown, to kill himself off early in the film. Directing and writing are his forte; Tarantino rightfully left the real acting to the professionals.

18. THE LAST SEDUCTION**** (1994)
110 minutes, Color

Director: John Dahl.
Producer: Jonathan Shestack.
Screenplay: Steve Barancik.
Photography: Jeffrey Jur.
Music: Joseph Vitarelli.
Editing: Eric L. Beason.
Stars: Linda Fiorentino, Peter Berg, Bill Pullman, J. T. Walsh, Bill Nunn.
Technicolor. HBO/Polygram/October Films. VHS: Polygram. DVD: Artisan.

Director John Dahl has created his own cottage industry out of film noir. He has made four films, three of which have made him the indisputable king of neo-noir—they are *Kill Me Again*, *Red Rock West*, and now *The Last Seduction*, Dahl's best neo-noir film to date. Linda Fiorentino stands alongside Barbara Stanwyck, in Billy Wilder's *Double Indemnity*; Jane Greer, in Jacques Tourneur's *Out of the Past*; and Kathleen Turner, in Lawrence Kasdan's *Body Heat*, as one of the greatest femmes fatales in film history. In fact, Fiorentino makes these dames seem like innocents—she is the ultimate man-eater and manipulator, as well as the prime mover, in Dahl's mystery/suspense thriller/black comedy.

The film opens in Manhattan. Bridget Gregory works as a telemarketing executive who manages a "stable" of telephone salesmen with leads to sell her products. The men are never as capable as she is and are constantly threatened by her no-nonsense masculine demeanor. Bridget is married to Clay Gregory, a medical student everyone calls "the doctor" because he illegally writes prescriptions for anyone who passes by with the right amount of cash. He has just scored some seven hundred thousand dollars in an illegal drug deal, selling medicinal cocaine to two black gangsters who first almost swindle him out of the cash, but then pay him off reluctantly. When Bridget returns home from work, Clay shows her the cash, and they intend to celebrate. They have a minor argument in which Clay slaps her face and then realizes he is wrong. Apologizing, he runs off into the shower while Bridget gathers up all the cash, picks up her car, and heads out of town. Clay watches her flee through an open window and vows he will have his revenge. Bridget is a dangerous woman, one you can never push over the edge. When Clay said to her, "Go, on, hit me harder," Bridget took the money and ran!

Driving to a small town near Buffalo called Beston, Bridget phones her lawyer, Frank Griffith (J. T. Walsh), who is aware of the theft. She asks him whether she should divorce her husband or kill him. The lawyer answers (with the best line in the entire film), "Hey lady, anyone check you for a heartbeat lately?" Bridget is as cold as ice, calculating, totally evil, spewing out venom, and using men as toys do to her bidding.

At a local bar in Beston (where she orders a Manhattan but cannot get served because she does not say "please"), Bridget meets Mike Swale (played as a nebbish by husky actor Peter Berg), a young guy recently divorced who has returned to the small town from Buffalo. Bridget discourages his advances at first and then abruptly encourages him to pursue her. She lays her plans spontaneously. She thinks Mike would be protection for her if her husband found her in Beston or sent some hoods to reclaim the cash she stole. She outrageously feels Mike's genitals and says to him straightforwardly, "Let's fuck." Unlike the 1940s films noirs like *Double Indemnity* or *The Big Sleep*, whose code restrictions forced the dialogue into double entendres, the new noir films are out in the open. *Chinatown*, *Body Heat*, and *Black Widow* have already exploited the freedom under the new rating system, and *The Last Seduction* follows in their tracks. Bridget and Mike are so hot for each other that barely undressed, she pins him to a fence as they copulate and reach orgasm. Bridget is the force that is completely in control of the situation.

On the following day, she changes her name to "Wendy Kroy," an anagram of "New York," her favorite city, and secures a job in a local insurance company. She warns the personnel officer of her ex-husband's extremely volatile nature, asking that her name and address be kept extremely confidential. Renting a house in town, she conspires with Mike to begin a business of murdering philandering husbands for cash, supplied by disgruntled wives who would like nothing better than to dispatch their mates and receive the insurance money. Bridget concocts this scheme using information about the insurance company's clients on the computer. Mike thinks she has gone bananas, but because he loves her, he will do anything for her. Big mistake! Bridget uses this grifter plan as a setup to see if Mike would be willing to murder her husband in New York.

Meanwhile, through a black private detective named Harlan (Bill Nunn), Clay discovers Wendy's whereabouts and sends the detective to reclaim the stolen cash. Wendy/Bridget cleverly kills Harlan, crashing her air-bagged car into a telephone pole while inveigling Harlan to show her his penis—"You know what they say about black men." Harlan, at his most vulnerable, doesn't have a chance; he goes headlong through the windshield. When Clay finds out about Harlan's death, he sends another private detective who stays in his own car, keeping Bridget under his surveillance. In a ploy to keep him from following her one day, she takes some store-bought cookies, heats them, and brings them out on a tray, under which she has carefully hidden a small board filled with pointed nails that she places under his rear tire as she "accidentally" drops a cookie. Fiorentino is wearing a very feminine, tiny apron, and brings the tray of cookies out walking in a very sexy, "Playboy bunny" fashion. Of course, when a taxi picks her up and the detective tries to follow, he is stymied in his attempt, realizing what a real bitch Fiorentino is. It is little touches of dry humor like this that make the film truly fun.

When in Buffalo, Bridget finds out Mike's secret—he apparently was married to a transvestite and came home with his tail between his legs. When Mike meets Wendy in the bar, he says to his male friends, "Fellas, with her, I am going to get my balls back!" And he almost does, except for the fact that Wendy/Bridget is a real castrating bitch and is never to be trusted.

The film winds up to an amazing conclusion. Wendy has told Mike all about her husband and her theft, and she devises a diabolical scheme to get rid of Clay once and for all. Mike will do anything for Bridget/Wendy, including murder her husband. But she tells Mike the mark is a man another woman wants out of the way, so they can cash in on their computer scheme. Mike arrives at Clay's apartment ready to kill him, but the latter talks him out of it. Clay realizes it is Bridget who is setting up this whole event and shows Mike a picture of them as man and wife. Mike suddenly realizes he has been duped. Mike and Bridget had agreed on a signal—he would shut out the lights after the deed had been done. Mike and Clay turn off the lights and await Bridget's arrival. She enters to find them both alive and even friendly. Thinking fast, Bridget takes a dispenser of mace and sprays it into Clay's mouth, forcing his mouth open as he lies tied up on the couch, and kills him. Mike is horrified but is so turned on sexually by Bridget that he begins to rape her as she calls the police, blaming him for the murder and the rape. In jail, Mike tells his attorney he is innocent and can only think of one detail that might prove it—the name card on the doorbell that Bridget changed so as not to give Mike a tip-off that the mark was really her husband. Cut to the next scene: Bridget has just come out of her old apartment building in upper Manhattan and disappears into a black limousine, holding the name card between her fingers and destroying it with a match. Obviously Bridget takes no prisoners and neglects no detail. Like Kathleen Turner in *Body Heat*, she uses the patsy, who is in jail for a long term, and escapes with the money, too.

The wonderful thing about *The Last Seduction* is the way actress Linda Fiorentino inhabits the role of Bridget/Wendy and takes control of the movie, going ahead full throttle. Casting her was brilliant, even inspired. We love to watch Fiorentino succeed because she always works outside of the law. Moreover, the old Hollywood morality is no longer at work here. We do not get a contrived conclusion in which she has to pay for her crimes. Fiorentino plays a self-serving bitch who goes all the way and comes out on top. She plays the role with relish, which gives the viewer a sense of liberation from the black-and-white films of the 1940s and 1950s. The script of *The Last Seduction* is titillating, ingenious, spiritually free, entertaining, and quite liberating. It is a breath of fresh air, and Fiorentino plays her role devastatingly—as if she was born to play Wendy Kroy. I especially like the way she tells any man exactly what he wants to hear and then continues with her own game plan, evil to the core. Fiorentino's character makes no pretenses: she is ferociously bad and only has a dark side. As George Cukor once said of Ava Gardner, "She is one of the best gentlemen I have ever known." We can say the same of Linda Fiorentino.

19. THE USUAL SUSPECTS**** (1995)
110 minutes, Color

Director: Bryan Singer.
Producers: Bryan Singer, Michael McDonnell.
Screenplay: Christopher McQuarrie.
Photography: Newton Thomas.
Music: John Ottman.
Editing: John Ottman.
Stars: Kevin Spacey, Stephen Baldwin, Gabriel Byrne, Benicio Del Toro, Chazz Palminteri, Kevin Pollak, Pete Postlethwaite.
Technicolor and Panavision. Polygram Films. VHS & DVD: Polygram (also in wide screen).

Bryan Singer's second film (after his debut with *Public Access* in 1993), is another heist film in the new noir style, borrowing much from the Coen brothers, Hitchcock, Scorsese, and especially Quentin Tarantino. This fluid film resembles Tarantino's *Reservoir Dogs* in one way—the use of refracted time, the insistence on multiple flashbacks to tell its labyrinthine story. And what a story it is!

Opening with a dockside explosion in present-time San Pedro, California, and the shooting death of Gabriel Byrne (as former corrupt cop Dean Keaton) by a known assailant, the film then cuts backward to explain what happened, showing the complex series of events leading up to the shooting. We learn it all started about six weeks previously with five criminals meeting in a lineup in New York City, accused of theft. They all claim to be innocent and decide to join forces on a job to take revenge on the police for picking them up. One job leads to another, and soon all of the men find themselves in way over their heads.

In present time, after the explosion on the boat thought to be carrying ninety-one million dollars in cocaine, we meet the two survivors. One is Verbal Kint (played by Spacey), a small-time con artist with a disfigured arm and a limp who tells customs agent Dave Kujan (his name, when pronounced in French, is *couillon*—"asshole") what he knows about the bombing and the plot that led to it. Spacey virtually narrates the film. In flashback, we learn how Verbal first met his co-conspirators in that fateful police lineup six weeks earlier. Besides former crooked cop Dean Keaton (Byrne), there were "hardware specialist" Todd Hockney (played with insouciance by Kevin Pollack), entry man Mike McManus (played angrily by Stephen Baldwin), and his nervous partner, Fenster (played by Benicio Del Toro), who cannot speak audibly. We learn Keaton wants to leave the crime scene and has a lawyer girlfriend named Edie Finneran (Suzie Amis) whom he adores; but he is sucked into his old life after trying to go straight in the investment business and losing his clients. All the men in the lineup need cash. Tipped by Mc-Manus that a drug-money drop is going down, the five, wearing stocking masks, hold up two cops and a bag man—the police surrender the dope and the cash. Although our group's heist is successful, a previously made phone call leads to the cops' and drug dealer's arrest and to the arrest of another fifty cops, including the precinct captain. Revenge is sweet!

Retreating to California for a short vacation to avoid investigation by the cops, another crook, named Redneck, asks if the group wants to work again; this time, the job is a jewelry heist in a skyscraper parking lot. The caper goes well, with all of the thieves surviving and killing their quarry. After fencing the emeralds, Redneck tells them he is working for someone named "Keyser Söze," that Söze brought them to California, and that they owe Söze big time for heists they pulled in the past that affected Söze's own business deals. Besides, Söze has a file on every member of the group, with their histories and records up to the present.

Not feeling intimidated, Fred Fenster (Benicio Del Toro) tries to run and is killed. The group buries the body in a shallow sandy grave on a California beach. Seeing that Söze's team means business, "the usual suspects"—Hockney, McManus, Kint, and Keaton—decide to show their own strength, kidnapping Kobayashi (Pete Postlethwaite with a heavy Oxford accent), Söze's second in command. Before they shoot him, however (they have just killed his two body-guards), Kobayashi reveals that Edie Finneran is working for Söze and is sitting in an office one floor below. Keaton, her former lover, checks this out and confirms it. The group realizes they must fulfill their pledge: to infiltrate a group of Argentine drug smugglers on a ship in San Pedro and take the ninety-one million dollars in cocaine as their bonus.

In another flashback, Verbal tells Keyser Söze's story: a Hungarian or Turkish mob tried to take over his territory, killing his children, raping his wife. Söze turned his gun on his own family first, killing his wife and several of his own children before he killed the invading gangsters, one by one. Thereafter, he killed every family member of that group and burned their homes and possessions. There was no being more diabolical than Keyser Söze, and Verbal fears him as well. Söze is an evil genius, perhaps the devil incarnate.

Customs Agent Kujan grills Verbal mercilessly, until we see what happened on the ship from his perspective. The five con men kill all of the Argentines, and Keaton, after going through every cabin, reveals he did not find one trace of cocaine. Moreover, everyone of the group is picked off, killed by a mysterious, tall man wearing a dark hat and overcoat. He stabs McManus to death with a knife in his neck; he shoots Keaton in the belly; he kills Pollack with a rifle blast as the former eyes a box full of cash hidden in the back of a truck parked on the dock. Only Verbal remains to tell the entire story. He reveals he saw this man murder his friends but was too paralyzed by fear to help any of them. The mysterious dark man then torched the entire boat, and some twenty-seven bodies were found aboard.

Since Verbal cannot be held by customs, he is released by Kujan (marvelously played by Chazz Palminteri). Verbal collects his belongings and starts walking out of the police station onto the street. Waiting for a fax of a sketch of Keyser Söze by the only other survivor of the massacre on the docked ship, Kujan looks at the bulletin board behind the desk where he and Verbal were sitting. He suddenly realizes from various clues—a news article about Guatemala, a sign saying the board was made in Skokie, Illinois (where Verbal said he had sung in a choir), and the bottom of a cup from a store called Kobayashi—that Verbal was spinning a tale, a whole series of lies. Kujan rushes out into the street looking for Verbal, who has quickened his pace with a suddenly straightened left leg and lit his own cigarette with a perfectly straight left arm, to be picked up in a black car by Kobayashi and driven off into infinity. Verbal says at the bitter end: "The greatest trick the devil ever pulled was convincing the world that he didn't exist . . . and just like that, poof, he was gone." When Kevin Spacey blows into his hand, the screen goes black and the end titles come up.

Director Bryan Singer appropriated the title of his film from the scene in Michael Curtiz's *Casablanca* (1942) in which Claude Rains says, " Round up the usual suspects." Singer's 1995 new noir triumph reeks of style and simplicity (despite a somewhat convoluted story). Most important is the ensemble acting by the usual suspects themselves. Gabriel Byrne is perfect as the former cop, a wistful dreamer with a kind of calm authority who has hopes of leaving the underworld for a better life with his beautiful lover. Stephen Baldwin is also excellent as a loud, comedic sociopath with a personality on the edge of unpredictability. Kevin Pollack, the Queens heist man, comes through with spunk, charm, and insouciance. His clashes with Baldwin are priceless shows of machismo and are brought to a halt when the gang tells them, "Now ladies, let's calm down." Benicio Del Toro adds a quirky accent and sometimes almost unfathomable speech that brings the film to a halt despite his unique sex appeal. Chazz Palminteri is terrific in his interrogation speeches as the customs agent who, we later discover, has been taken for a ride throughout the film. Pete Postlethwaite's Oxford accent is matched by his servile demeanor and loyalty to his master, Kayser Söze. Kevin Spacey, as

Verbal Kint, plays most of the film with a shadowy cowardice and an inno-cence, supposedly true to his feelings and very observant, worthy of our sym-pathy and admiration—until we discover he is the real villain, as well as a very unreliable narrator.

The Usual Suspects is a fluid film, a tease with wonderful style. Sometimes, like Howard Hawks's *The Big Sleep* (1946), it may not make much sense. You have to pay attention to the details, which are sometimes subsumed by its velvety style. But the film is quite linear, and there is beauty in its simplicity despite the seemingly intricate nature of its plot. The twist at the end is a real corker—we never suspect that Spacey's sly intelligence, behind that ineffec-tual pose, is working full-time to deceive the viewer. And when we discover his true identity, we rethink all the events in the film, which, several days later, still stays in the mind. Although at times the events defy logic, and some clues are revealed gradually while others remain hidden, on a second or third viewing, *The Usual Suspects* is always fresh and entertaining. And that wonderful new noirish musical score by the film's editor, John Ottman, keeps the film moving mysteriously to its fabulous conclusion! It is too bad the end titles do not return to the shimmering, shadowy, dark ripples of ocean water with the harbor's lamplight reflected on its surface. This wonderful noir touch behind the opening credit gets you in the mood and keeps you there for nearly two hours. *The Usual Suspects* is one of the best new noirs of the decade, and one hopes Bryan Singer and John McQuarrie will collaborate again and bring us more films in the same style with their usual expertise.

20. L.A. CONFIDENTIAL**** (1997)
138 minutes, Color

Director: Curtis Hanson.
Producers: Curtis Hanson, Arnon Milchan.
Screenplay: Curtis Hanson, Brian Helgeland, based on the James Ellroy novel.
Photography: Dante Spinotti.
Music: Jerry Goldsmith.
Editing: Peter Honess.
Stars: Russell Crowe, Guy Pearce, Kevin Spacey, James Cromwell, Kim Basinger, Danny DeVito.
Technicolor and Panavision. Warner Bros. VHS & DVD: Warner Bros. (released in a wide-screen version).

If it were not for James Cameron's gargantuan film *Titanic,* with all of its thrilling special effects, *L.A. Confidential* would have been named best picture of the year by the American Motion Picture Academy of Arts and Sciences. As far as this author is concerned, it *is* the best picture of 1997!

If the adjective "labyrinthine" has been overused to describe the plots of recent neo-noir films, it is only appropriate to apply it again to most of the new noir films of the decade of the 1990s—and *L.A. Confidential* certainly qualifies, with its intricate story based on an even more complex novel. Complexity is the key word for the new noir films, a truism which is "off the record, on the QT, and very much hush-hush," to borrow a leitmotif from the film.

Set in the early 1950s in Los Angeles, the film has multiple layers of plot and characterization that finally dovetail to reveal a startling conclusion with all threads of the story neatly tied up. The screenwriters' tight script is masterful and among the best ever written in the noir style. "It is paradise on earth . . . that's what they tell you, anyway," begins Sid Hudgens (Danny DeVito), as grainy color pictures of the utopia known as Los Angeles in the 1950s flash past the viewer's eyes. Swimming pools, no snow, and all the oranges you can eat—a fantasy of the post–World War II era, when everyone went west in quest of the American dream. But when you look closer, there is rot, crime, and corruption in this "paradise on earth"— and Sid Hudgens, publisher of the well-known tabloid *Hush-Hush* (based on *Confidential Magazine*) is marketing the dirt, the underbelly of Hollywood's glitter.

We first meet detective Jack Vincennes (masterfully played by Kevin Spacey), who is Hudgens's main contact in the smut exposure market. When

Vincennes makes a bust, especially for illegal possession of marijuana (his real-life counterpart reputedly busted Robert Mitchum) or sexual indiscretions, Hudgens—who pays Vincennes off—is on the spot with his camera. Hudgens lives off the cops who give him information to boost the circulation of his tawdry magazine. Vincennes is a snappy dresser and technical adviser to a *Dragnet*-like television show, which gives him a sort of celebrity among the cops. The director told Spacey two words that helped him develop his characterization: "Dean Martin." Spacey moves and dresses just like the 1950s movie star/singer, but adds a touch of previously undiscovered morality: Vincennes realizes he has lost his self-respect because of his participation in the *Hush-Hush* scams and scandals.

Introduced next is sergeant Edmund Exley, son of one of Los Angeles's most revered detectives (marvelously played by Australian actor Guy Pearce), who wears glasses and always acts by the book. Exley is prissy and a spoilsport, despised by everyone in the precinct because of his moral fiber and straight-arrow philosophy about finding the truth behind all events. Finally, the third detective, also Australian and playing an American cop, is Bud White (brilliantly acted by Russell Crowe), whose approach to duty is that of a hard-drinking, hard-brawling cop—the savior of women who are the victims of violence. His exterior is rough, but underneath, he is a sweet, plodding sort of guy until violence turns him into a raging brute. None of the three detectives particularly like each other. Vincennes is resented because of his television ties; no one likes Exley because of his college training; and everyone hates Bud because he is a hothead prone to violence.

However, all three men cross paths because of a singular event—the Night Owl Cafe murders in downtown Los Angeles. On Christmas Eve, during a party at the precinct, a group of Mexicans is brought to jail, supposedly for beating two cops. White's partner, Dick Stensland (Graham Beckel), is fairly drunk and initiates a riot in the station house cellblock, in which even Vincennes's shirt is bloodied and Exley, trying to prevent the beatings, is forced into a cell. The press is present, and so disparaging headlines appear the next morning in the Los Angeles papers, citing police brutality. Present at the riot is captain Dudley Smith (excellently played by James Cromwell), who asks Exley if he has the guts to shoot a man in the back, knowing he is guilty of a heinous crime but will get off because of the complexity of the laws and the artfulness of defense lawyers. Exley answers that he only plays by the book.

Arriving late to the jailhouse riot is Bud White. While buying some liquor for the police party, he meets Lynn Bracken, a Veronica Lake look-alike, dressed in a black-hooded silk coat that makes her look fabulously beautiful. As Lynn places her order, White leaves and notices in a chauffeur-driven car (the driver is an ex-cop named Leland Meeks, played by Darrell Sanders) a woman with facial bandages sitting next to an elegant society dude named Pierce Patchett (played by David Strathairn). White begins to interrogate Patchett. Lynn emerges from the liquor store and interrupts, saying, "It's not what you think, officer." The car is driven away after White is assured that no harm has been done to the bandaged girl.

All of this is preparation for the Night Owl Cafe murders. Two of the victims are Dick Stensland, White's ex-partner who incited the violence in the jail the night before and was summarily fired from the force, and the girl with the bandaged face, a Rita Hayworth look-alike. Exley and Captain Smith investigate the murders—which leads them to a group of black men with shotguns sequestered in a garage-parked car. They are rounded up and jailed, which in turn leads to another subplot—the rape of a Mexican woman by an unarmed black man, who is notoriously killed by White, planting a gun in the victim's hand. But Exley and White are not happy about the resolution of the Night Owl Cafe massacre. It is too easy and circumstantial to cast blame on the black men. And what was Stensland doing with a woman identified as Sue Lefferts, the Rita Hayworth look-alike, in that café on that particular evening?

Bud White traces Lynn Bracken back to her home. She admits that she is a highly paid prostitute and works for Pierce Patchett as a sometime actress (his Veronica Lake look-alike), and Bud begins to fall in love with her. At the same time, drug kingpin Mickey Cohen is jailed, and some of his henchmen are murdered when they try to take over Mickey's turf. These events seem incidental until we discover twenty-five pounds of heroin have disappeared from a drug bust and that Stensland was trying to sell it. Stensland was a friend of another ex-cop, Leland Meeks, who chauffeured Pierce Patchett the evening Bud White first met Lynn at the liquor store. Moreover, when White appears at Sue Leffert's house, finding out Stensland was her boyfriend, he also uncovers Meeks's rotting body in the basement of her home. It seems that Stensland and Meeks were dealing heroin, and were trying to cross the Mickey Cohen mob for the profits—and were killed because of it.

However, there are several loose ends to these crimes. Jack Vincennes discovers that captain Dudley Smith signed all the police reports having to do with the investigations of the drug busts. One evening Vincennes shows up at Dudley Smith's home and innocently asks the captain about his participation. Smith surprisingly shoots Vincennes, who utters the name "Rolo Tommasi" and dies. Vincennes's death is one of the best scenes actor Kevin Spacey has ever played. You can see the lights go out in his eyes. Apparently Dudley Smith has been taking over Los Angeles as a kingpin criminal, since

Mickey Cohen is in jail, and Meeks and Stensland were part of a group of corrupt cops cashing in on the flow of heroin. But the two cops were greedy, and Smith had them killed.

When Vincennes's body is found in Echo Park, Smith asks Exley to investigate the case and questions him about another lead: "Did you ever hear the name Rolo Tommasi?" It is at this point Exley realizes Smith is Vincennes's murderer; Exley made up that name, an anonymous person who murdered his father, and Vincennes was the only other person who knew it. Meanwhile, Smith feels the heat is on and starts to tie up loose ends.

Smith, acting in his capacity of captain and vigilante cop, asks Bud White to come out to the Victory Motel to work over a few criminals. One of them is Sid Hudgens, who has taken some incriminating photographs of Exley fornicating with Lynn Bracken. When White sees them, he flies into a rage. He goes to the police station and starts to beat Exley. Here Exley reveals that Smith is the murderer of Vincennes and wants Exley dead because he suspects Exley is onto him. White listens to reason, and he and Exley go to the district attorney, Ellis Loew (played by Ron Rifkin), asking for wiretaps and bank records on Captain Smith. Loew refuses, but White plays bad cop with him and practically tosses him out of a window until he admits to his complicity in the crimes. It seems Patchett has blackmailed a local councilman with indiscreet photos of him in bed with Lynn Brackett. Then Loew admits he is a homosexual and was seduced by a young actor named Matt, played by Simon Baker Eddy, and photographed in bed with the actor. Matt was also murdered because he knew about Dudley Smith's scheme to take over the dope racket—found with his throat slit at a Los Angeles motel by Vincennes.

Realizing Smith is on a rampage to cover up his crimes, Exley and White go to Pierce Patchett's home and find him drugged with his wrists slit, having bled to death. Realizing Lynn Bracken may be in danger, White sends Exley to insure her safety. White does not want to face Lynn because he beat her up in a previous scene, when he saw photos of her with Exley. Lynn is fine but knows nothing about Smith. Meanwhile White discovers Hudgens beaten to death in his office—he had seen Hudgens previously at the Victory Motel. White realizes now he was set up by Smith, who then murdered Hudgens. Receiving a call from headquarters, supposedly from Exley, White is summoned to the Victory Motel. He meets Exley there, and they realize they were told to meet there, but *not* by each other.

The last five or six minutes of the film consist of a terrifically played shoot-out between Exley and White on one side and Captain Smith and his band of rogue cops on the other. At the end, Smith nearly kills White, who shoves a dagger into Smith's leg as he is about to kill Exley. White has pushed

Exley out of the way of Smith's shotgun blast, ultimately saving his life. As Exley gets the drop on Smith and the latter begins to walk out of the motel toward the sound of police sirens and oncoming headlights, Exley shoots Smith in the back, killing him. If he had not done it, Smith would have talked himself out of the punishment for his crimes.

The final scene shows Exley receiving a second award for bravery and Lynn leading him to a car where White is bandaged and in an arm cast. Lynn tells Exley they are going to Arizona, to her hometown of Bisbee, and will have each other. Exley says, "Thanks for the push" to White; they shake hands, and Exley watches the car drive off into the distance.

As the end titles roll, a small surprise is watching Hopalong Cassidy on horseback in a parade, waving to a crowd and closely followed by district attorney Ron Rifkin and the star of the *Dragnet*-styled television show *Badge of Honor*. As the roll up ends, there is another surprise: the opening titles of the same television show and a dedication to detective Jack Vincennes. The director is having his way with the audience, entertaining us with these ironic codas until the very end of the titles.

L.A. Confidential is probably one of the best neo-noirs ever made. Even James Ellroy was supremely happy with Curtis Hanson and Brian Helgeland's adaptation from his huge and intractable novel. But most important, Hanson cast the film to perfection. Kevin Spacey is exactly right in the role of Jack Vincennes and has a wonderful screen presence.

When Arnon Milchan, the producer, heard that two Australian actors were going to play leading roles in an American film, dealing with Los Angeles of the 1950s, he wondered if Russell Crowe and Guy Pearce could really do the job. He was amazed by their terrific performances. Crowe is especially good at switching from his calm-guy to his mean-guy demeanor, and Pearce is excellent playing a good cop with softer edges, ambitious and a pariah, refusing to cover up for corrupt cops in his precinct. Both actors expertly developed American accents to cover their own tangy Aussie dialects.

Of the other principals, James Cromwell is extraordinarily good playing the well-liked but extremely evil captain Dudley Smith. He receives his just desserts when Exley murders him at the finale, something Smith thought the moral college boy incapable of. And of course, Kim Basinger as Lynn Bracken steals the film from every actor. She inhabits her role with every correct word and gesture. Her acting is so genuine that Curtis Harrington felt she had been perfectly cast.

Turning to some of the other supporting actors, David Strathairn was cast perfectly as Pierce Patchett, a Los Angeles millionaire who, through blackmail, corrupts a councilman to change his vote for building the Santa Monica Freeway, which would make Patchett even richer. Just as in Roman Polanski's 1974 film *Chinatown*, to which this film is often compared, there is a real political subtext here. In Polanski's film, it is water rights and the illegal buying of land; in *L.A. Confidential*, it is racketeering in drugs and highway construction. Strathairn acquits himself well as a man who is rich and wants to be richer. Pimping and producing B movies are not enough for him.

Also, Paul Guilfoyle, who, as Mickey Cohen, has less than ten minutes of screen time, plays his role wonderfully. His image of a corrupt drug dealer and ladies' man is very memorable. There are other actors too numerous to name who make significant contributions—as Lana Turner and Johnny Stompanato look-alikes, for example. To be counted among the stars are the photographer, Dante Spinotti—who photographed the film in a realistic white light, not the stylistic shadows of the earlier noir films—and the production designer, Jeannine Claudia Oppenwall—who re-created the costumes and objects of the 1950s so faithfully (with Ruth Myers) that even a Coke bottle or a pack of Chesterfield cigarettes looks exactly as it did in that era. And finally, there is Jerry Goldsmith's wonderful underscoring. With a trumpet used in the major themes, there are echoes of Chet Baker and Bobby Troop's famous sounds, combined with source music of the period: for example, Kay Starr's great song "Wheel of Fortune," Dean Martin's "Smile," and Johnny Mercer's "Accentuate the Positive," among many others.

It is also interesting that two films dealing with corruption and murder in Los Angeles had appeared the year before: Lee Tamahori's *Mulholland Falls* and Carl Franklin's *Devil in a Blue Dress*. Both are neo-noir and will be noted in this book's filmography. But both films did not do well critically because they were not tightly written or directed. Besides having a great script and a look of gritty reality, *L.A. Confidential* is brilliant filmmaking—perhaps the best detective neo-noir thriller made since Orson Welles's death knell to film noir, the equally brilliant *Touch of Evil* (1958). *L.A. Confidential* is an intelligent film, consistently engaging, insightful, artful, and an homage to the film noir masterpieces of the 1940s and 1950s. It is beautifully realized and gives us a wonderful idea of what life must have been like in the glamorous and sleazy underworld of 1950s Los Angeles. It redefines the classic contours of film noir, catching us up in the faded 1950s beauty of Los Angeles. To reiterate, it is probably the best modern noir film ever made.

21. MEMENTO** (2000)
113 minutes, B&W and Color

Director: Christopher Nolan.
Producers: Jennifer Todd, Suzanne Todd.
Screenplay: Christopher Nolan, Jonathan Nolan, based on Jonathan Nolan's short story "Memento Mori."
Photography: Willy Pfister.
Music: David Julyan.
Editing: Dody Dorn.
Stars: Guy Pearce, Carrie-Anne Moss, Joe Pantoliano.
Newmarket Films. VHS & DVD: Newmarket.

Memento stars Guy Pearce as Leonard Shelby, a young man whose wife, Catherine (played by Jorja Fox), was raped and murdered. Shelby suffers from short-term memory loss and uses notes and tattoos on his body to hunt down his wife's killer. Although memory and the manipulation of it are key to the film, *Memento* is a fascinating exercise in new-noir style. It proceeds backward in time until the actual murder is witnessed by Shelby, and we discover the real perpetrator: Joe Pantoliano as Teddy Grammell. It is not the discovery of "whodunit" that makes the film fascinating, but Leonard Shelby's memory loss and his constant desire for revenge.

Leonard uses a series of annotated Polaroid snapshots to track down the killer as the film moves backward in time. Some critics may feel this method of storytelling is innovative in structure. It took me two screenings to figure out how Christopher Nolan filmed and edited his story—he used three- to eight-minute scene segments, each one beginning where the previous scene ended. Confusing? Certainly! Do we enter easily into the mindset of the character? No. There are too many cryptic clues and red herrings that derail the story line.

The finale of the film is predictable and logical. There is no plot twist but a series of revelations leading us to an ambiguous conclusion. We wonder if the characters played by Carrie-Anne Moss and Joe Pantoliano are really telling us the truth as they reveal the roles they played in the murder of Catherine Shelby. Most film critics have lionized this film because of its supposed innovative style. I have included *Memento* in this section because of its challenging style, allowing for multiple interpretations by its viewers. This muddled film about murder and revenge is one of a spate of new noirs starting off the new millennium. And certainly Guy Pearce's outstanding performance is worth the price of admission. When *Memento*'s producers, Newmarket Films, presented it at the Sundance Film Festival in 2001, it was a bleak movie-going season. Nolan's film was cheered on by critics who were looking for an art-house work of cinematic style. It is too bad *Memento* is not as artful as it presumes to be. Christopher Nolan is certainly a fine English director with much talent. In the true spirit of neo-noir, he has made more original films, some of them successful remakes that show off his extraordinary talent.

22. SEXY BEAST**** (2000)
88 minutes, Color

Director: Jonathan Glazer.
Producer: Jeremy Thomas.
Screenplay: Louis Mellis, David Scinto.
Photography: Ivan Bird.
Music: Roque Bannos.
Editing: John Scott, Sam Sneade.
Stars: Ray Winstone, Ben Kingsley, Ian McShane, James Fox.
DeLuxe Color/Super. Fox Searchlight Pictures/Films Four 35. VHS & DVD: Fox.

From England, this film is the part of a wave of British new noirs (*Get Carter* [1971], *The Long Good Friday* [1975], and *The Limey* [1999] also come to mind). It is the first of its kind to succeed in the United States at the box office. Ray Winstone (a British actor virtually unknown to American audiences) stars as Gal, a retired safecracker living in southern Spain on the Costa del Sol with his wife, Deedee (played by Amanda Redman); they share their lives with another Brit retired racketeering couple, Aitch and Jackie (Cavan Kendall and Julianne White). They are visited by Don Logan, played by none other than Ben Kingsley—"the most savage mad-dog frothing gangster in recent movies," says Roger Ebert in his review at www.Chicago-SunTimes.com. Don wants Gal to pull off one last caper in London, a safecracking job for Teddy (Ian McShane), who is sexually involved with Harry (Edward Fox), an upper-crust English bank owner whose safe is targeted for theft. When Gal refuses to go back with Don to London, all hell breaks loose. Don becomes like a pit bull, tough and ugly. He refuses to take no for an answer and succeeds in so thoroughly insulting Gal and Deedee that Gal reluctantly returns for one last job.

What we do not notice is the dislocation of time in the film's narrative, which affects the way brutal, violent events are finally revealed. Director Jonathan Glazer, in his debut film, has followed admirably the twisty script written by Louis Mellis and David Scinto. The story is like a three-act play. In act 1, Gal is swimming in his private pool when a huge boulder comes rolling furiously down a hillside, barely missing Gal as it lands in the middle of the pool, damaging the bottom. What an opening scene! It is a prescient moment. Then Don arrives fomenting violence through insults, threatening Gal and his wife, creating a dangerous and frightening situation at their retirement villa.

Act 2 begins with Gal's return to London. We discover Teddy's plan is to rob his lover's bank by drilling into a vault containing safe-deposit boxes from a pool inside a Turkish bath next door to the bank. One box, opened during the heist, contains a surprise—a pack of cigarettes that Teddy placed there so he could case the job unsuspected by his lover. Gal steals some earrings for Deedee from another safe-deposit box, revealing his soft side for the love of his life. The brutality continues after the heist when Teddy murders his lover Harry, the banker—the only link between Teddy and the crime. Gal flies back to Spain.

Act 3 contains the resolution of the Don-Gal conflict. We watch Don return to Gal's house after being forced off an Iberian jetliner when he refuses to stop smoking. Don's brutalization of Gal and particularly Deedee worsens, and so they murder him with a shotgun. Teddy discovers Don is missing, perhaps dead, as he drives Gal to the airport. "No," says Gal, "Don disappeared," and thus neither Gal nor Don will receive a share of the profits from the heist. The mob is willing to let Gal go home and forget about Don's murder or disappearance. We also watch a Ben Kingsley look-alike in Don's nightmare, in the form of a prancing animal, rabbitlike, perhaps the "sexy beast" of the title. (Kingsley is certainly a beast, but *not* sexy!) Kingsley is masterful in this role, and the film closes on a happy but ironic note.

Everyone gets what they want except Don. This neo-noir for the twenty-first century contains the criminal elements, brutality, and violence. It is a caper film of a successful bank heist gone wrong in certain ways and a disappeared hit man, set in gorgeous locales but with a harrowing, twisty plot that will unnerve the viewer.

23. THE DEEP END**** (2001)
100 minutes, Color

Directors: Scott McGehee, David Siegel.
Producers: Scott McGehee, David Siegel.
Screeplay: Scott McGehee, David Siegel.
Photography: Giles Nuttgens.
Music: Peter Nashel.
Editing: Lauren Zuckerman.
Stars: Tilda Swinton, Goran Visnjic, Jonathan Tucker, Peter Donat.
CinemaScope. Fox-Searchlight Pictures. VHS & DVD: Fox.

The remake of a 1947 black-and-white film noir directed by Max Ophuls—
The Reckless Moment, starring Joan Bennett and James Mason—*The Deep End* is in beautiful color, shot luxuriously on location in Lake Tahoe. Both films are based on a *Saturday Evening Post* story from a novel by Elisabeth Sanxay entitled *The Blank Wall.* In both films, Margaret Hall, the mother played by Brit actress Tilda Swinton, is the heroic yet vulnerable mother figure, willing to sacrifice home and hearth to save her child from a murder conviction. Both films involve blackmail.

In the 1948 version, James Mason plays Donnelly, an Irish thug who has gotten hold of Joan Bennett's daughter's incriminating love letters to a married man (Sheppard Strudwick)—who, while drunk, accidentally falls off their lakeside dock and impales himself on a beached anchor. In the 2001 version, directed by Scott McGehee, Goran Visnjic plays Alek Spera, a Slavic blackmailer who has gotten hold of an incriminating videotape showing Tilda Swinton's son, Beau (played by Jordan Tucker), in a homosexual act with Darby Reese (menacingly played by Josh Lucas). Darby, too, drunkenly and accidentally falls on an anchor and bleeds to death, setting into motion the noirish events of the film.

These mothers' love knows no bounds when it comes to protecting their children. In Joan Bennett's case, she almost falls in love with the James Mason blackmailer character, who dies in an auto accident, surrendering the incriminating letters that will save her daughter's reputation and avoid a murder charge.

In the Tilda Swinton version, she tries to finagle the blackmail money (twenty-five thousand dollars) for Spera. He comes to admire this courageous, feminist mother who is willing to go to any lengths to protect her gay son. Spera kills his own boss in a fight in a boathouse, and Spera is mortally wounded. Spera then dies in a self-made auto accident, surrendering the incriminating videotape to Tilda Swinton, with whom he has fallen in love.

In the 1948 version, Bennett's husband is overseas, somewhere in the South Pacific, during World War II, leading to the daughter's "reckless moment"—her affair with a married man. There was some contemporary urgency to this story, with the father figure absent and unable to provide moral support. Bennett is left to hold her postwar American home together and enact *both* the role of mother and that of father. Tilda Swinton's husband is also on a military mission, on an aircraft carrier somewhere in the mid-Atlantic, but her life seems more luxurious in the Lake Tahoe setting. Both women need to rely on the kindness of strangers, since their husbands are away on military duty. Nevertheless, the entire plot of both films turns on the accidental death of a man and a mother's determination to sequester the body in a nearby body of water.

The Deep End (2001) updates the original novel with a gay theme. The bar owned by Darby Reese, whom Beau Hall is attracted to, is called the Deep End—a gay club in Reno. And it is in the deep end of Lake Tahoe that Darby is anchored until the body unexpectedly surfaces. The police investigation of the homicide that follows ends inconclusively in both films, because both blackmailers sacrifice themselves for the platonic love and admiration of the protective mother figure.

The most important noirish element in the film is the practiced way Tilda Swinton, as Margaret Hall, keeps secrets. She hides the body of her son's lover, drives the latter's car back to Reno, and wipes off her fingerprints from the steering wheel and doors. She hides her son's foray into a homosexual affair from her father-in-law, Jack Hall (played by Peter Donat), who lives with them, not revealing her assumption that her son killed his lover and her own guilt in having hidden the body—she may be an accomplice to murder!

Tilda Swinton is completely absorbing and marvelous in the mother role—desperate, harassed by her children, loving, devoted, juggling her daily routines of music lessons, ballet classes, and swimming at her health club (her only private moment). She covers up a possible murder, is sought after by blackmailers, tries to secure bank loans, pawns jewelry, deals with her father-in-law's heart attack, picks up the children from various schools and lessons, *and* does the laundry and prepares all the meals! Into this everyday life, neo-noir villainy intrudes, which makes *The Deep End* an exceptionally involving, intelligent thriller. In an odd way, it is a love story, too. It deals with mother love, the fiercest love of all, asking how far a mother will go to protect her son (or daughter) from the evils in the world. The villains themselves do not have much heart for their task of blackmail after meeting the mother character in the film's two versions, but they cannot let the task go once the dark wheels of the plot have been set into motion. *The Deep End* is an intense neo-noir thriller that grabs its audience and does not let us go.

24. IN THE BEDROOM**** (2001)
131 minutes, Color

Director: Todd Field.
Producers: Todd Field, Ross Katz, Graham Leader.
Screenplay: Todd Field, Roger Festiger, based on the Andre Dubus story "Killings."
Photography: Antonio Calavache.
Music: Thomas Newman.
Editing: Frank Reynolds.
Stars: Tom Wilkinson, Sissy Spacek, Marisa Tomei, Nick Stahl, William Mapother.
Technicolor. Good Machine Films. VHS & DVD: Miramax

Much like *The Deep End, In the Bedroom* involves a contemporary American family, this time in Maine (the film was shot entirely in the town of Camden). The young son, Frank Fowler (played by Nick Stahl), is having a hot-blooded, summertime affair with divorcée Natalie Strout (Marisa Tomei in one of her finest roles) against the will of his parents, Matt and Ruth Fowler (played by Tom Wilkinson and Sissy Spacek, the latter in one of her best and most illuminating roles since *Carrie* [1976] or *Coal Miner's Daughter* [1980]).

The Deep End and *In the Bedroom* share three themes: family problems that lead to drastic actions; the way overprotective mothers can alienate their children and change their children's destinies; and the shared secrets and clandestine actions of the characters. All this leads to unexpected noirish violence and brutality when criminals are placed beyond the reach of the law.

The film opens in a small New England town, where Ruth Fowler is the choral director in the local high school, and her husband Matt is the town doctor. Their son, Frank, in his early twenties and supposedly going off to an Ivy League law school in the fall, is having a romance with divorced Natalie Strout. Frank is more in love with the idea of being in love, and Matt, vicariously enjoys his son's sexual conquest of this older nubile woman. Ruth just watches the situation unfold, aware that her husband is enthralled with the young lovers. Her controlling nature makes it difficult to have her son retreat from her in this romantic summer interlude, but says nothing. She intuits, however, her son's real passion for this divorced woman in her thirties with two small children and that he will probably become a local fisherman because of the relationship, dashing all her hopes of Frank's becoming an eminent lawyer. Added to the familial mix of personalities is Richard Strout (stunningly played by handsome newcomer William Mapother), who wishes to reconcile with his ex-wife and two children and is cognizant of her current affair with Frank.

The second part of the film focuses on a sudden, violent explosion. Frank tries to protect Natalie from her former abusive husband, who is visiting his children; Richard shoots and kills Frank in a rage and stalks wildly out of his former home. Natalie collapses, holding her dying young lover in her arms, and then sends for the local police. Frank's parents are distraught with their loss.

Natalie approaches Ruth, offering her condolences, but Ruth explodes in a moment of violence, slapping Natalie resoundingly hard because of her role in Frank's murder. Richard is brought to trial but claims the shooting was an accident, since there was no eyewitness—although we viewers actually see it was a violent murder. He is freed after a short trial.

Camden is a very small town, and the Fowlers run into Richard Strout at the local bar, in the local supermarket, and elsewhere. He is the local rich kid who got away with his crime because his father runs the largest fish-canning company in town. In their private moments, Ruth argues with Matt, accusing him of living through their son's sexuality vicariously. Matt accuses his wife of having a controlling nature regarding their own marriage and their son's upbringing. Ruth and Matt feel they are the real victims and justice has not been served. It is here, in the bedroom, that Matt silently dreams of a way to save his marriage, now undergoing the hardest challenge to its survival.

In the last part of the film, Matt follows Richard to the latter's apartment one very late night and, at gunpoint, tells him to get out of town. Ruth is troubled by seeing Richard on an almost daily basis. Matt shows Richard a train ticket he bought for him and pointedly leaves it in Richard's apartment; Richard agrees to go. Then, accompanied by Matt's best friend, the men drive into a Maine forest and stop at a deserted area where Matt had previously dug a grave. He shoots Richard to death, and both men bury him in the dead of night. The friends separate and Matt returns before dawn to his wife. As they prepare for bed, she asks him, "Is it done?" He nods. Now life will go on more easily for the Fowlers, who share their dream of revenge and retribution for the unfortunate death of their son Frank.

In the Bedroom is director Todd Field's debut film, based on a short story by Andre Dubus. All the actors play their roles perfectly in this beautifully lighted, brilliantly Technicolored film with a daylight Maine locale. But one can never forget the dark side of these characters. Marisa Tomei is as dangerously alluring as any femme fatale of the 1940s. William Mapother, playing her ex-husband, is just as brutal as any hit man of the same era. Tom Wilkinson, who executes the murderer, and Sissy Spacek, his wife, who shares in his dream of vengeance, are the real new noir characters; they have committed a murder and are going to the end of the line, whatever the consequences. We hope they get away with it—a real twist on 1940s morality in the new millennium. And while recent neo-noir films tend to sympathize with the criminal, this one is the first of the new noirs to sensitively and intelligently deal with the *victims* of a crime and their feelings.

25. THE MAN WHO WASN'T THERE**** (2001)
116 minutes, B&W

Director: Joel Coen.
Producer: Ethan Coen.
Screenplay: Joel Coen, Ethan Coen.
Photography: Roger Deakins.
Music: Carter Burwell.
Editing: Roderick Jaynes (Ethan and Joel Coen), Tricia Cooke.
Stars: Billy Bob Thornton, Frances McDormand, James Gandolfini, Michael Badalucco, Scarlett Johansson, Tony Shalhoub.
CinemaScope. Working Title Films. VHS & DVD: USA Entertainment.

The Coen brothers, Joel and Ethan, have done it again. Their first wonderful foray into neo-noir territory was *Blood Simple*, in 1983; their latest return to neo-noir is a complete sendup of the original noir style of the 1940s called *The Man Who Wasn't There*, a prize winner at the Cannes Film Festival of 2001. The film is photographed in gorgeous black and white with elegant shades of gray, using a combination of light and shadows to tell its twisty noir story. It has the perfect noir prototype loser in Billy Bob Thornton as Ed Crane, a small-town California barber who narrates the entire film in a passive style. His voice-over describes his alcoholic wife, Doris (the femme fatale), and her affair with her boss, "Big" Dave Brewster, owner of the Nirdlinger Department Store (ironic name for a trio of misfits!).

Ed narrates the ancient story of greedy and murderous pursuits in a world of cigarette smoke and deep moral turpitude. Thornton is exactly right as the passive husband who wants to get out of his marriage to his two-timing shrew of a wife. He launches a scheme to defraud her boss, Big Dave, out of ten thousand dollars by writing the latter an anonymous blackmail note saying, "Everyone will know what you've been up to." Dave pays off the anonymous writer, leaving the money in a case in a fleabag hotel.

Ed collects it and invests it as seed money in a start-up dry cleaning business, shares of which are sold to him by a grifter, Creighton Tolliver (played unctuously by Jon Polito). But the grifter runs out on Ed with the cash, and Big Dave discovers it was Ed who blackmailed him. In a fight between the men, Ed accidentally kills Dave, but since he had no discernible motive for the crime, he is not considered a suspect. However, Doris is arrested because her affair with Dave was not exactly sub-rosa, and the police discover accounting shortages in her boss's books. (She was the head accountant for the Nirdlinger Department Store.) Doris is wrongly accused of the murder since she had the only motive to kill Big Dave. Besides, it is later revealed she is pregnant with Dave's child. Ed confesses to the police, but they don't believe him. He hires a big-time lawyer, Freddie Reidenschneider (wonderfully played by Tony Shalhoub), to defend his wife.

Freddie says: "I am a lawyer. You are a barber. You know *nothing!*" ("Reidenschneider" is the name of the archvillain who designs the heist [actor Sam Jaffee] in John Huston's ultimate heist noir film, *The Asphalt Jungle* [1950]—no coincidence here!] Doris is convicted of a murder she did not commit and hangs herself in her cell, fearing Ed's wrath when he finds out about her pregnancy. Apparently they had not been lovers for years!

Ed returns to the barbershop chair, chain-smoking, working with his brother-in-law Frank Raffo (superbly played by Michael Badalucco), trapped into a life so bad he wants to *scream*, until he meets Birdy Abundes (Scarlet Johansson), a teenage pianist. For Ed, she represents innocence, youth, beauty, and, above all, talent. He is willing to sponsor her lessons and career, for which Birdy is more than grateful, willing to show her affection by performing an act of fellatio while Ed is driving, to which his reaction is, "Oh, my, heavens to Betsy!" Ed really has lost his innocence and belief in a pure woman after this incident.

But the real punch in the plot comes when the body of the grifter, Tolliver, is found underwater in a local river; Ed is arrested for his murder after the police link Ed to the man in another investigation. The killer was probably Big Dave, who was also conned by Tolliver, but Ed is jailed for life and resolutely accepts his fate in a voice-over. (The twist probably derived from the finale of James M. Cain's oft-filmed novel *The Postman Always Rings Twice*, in which Frank Chambers *does* kill Cora's husband, Nick, but is blamed for Cora's death in a freak auto accident, since he has the only discernible motive.)

Billy Bob Thornton has the role of his life as the man who wasn't there. His chain-smoking, laconic narration, craggy features, and large, sunken, staring eyes all attest to his passive, indolent nature; he is a man trapped in a life he hates but from which he cannot liberate himself. His inaction, his mournful sensibility, his indifference contribute to the sendup of this ultimate noir loser. He even resolves most of his problems in social situations by smoking!

Frances McDormand is equally terrific as the not-so-pretty alcoholic wife who believes she *is* a femme fatale. In one scene she is lying supposedly nude in a bathtub. She asks Billy Bob to shave her legs; she lies there sexily as he, with cigarette dangling at the corner of his mouth, passively and reluctantly accedes to her command. Obviously, there is no sexual connection between them.

James Gandolfini as Big Dave, trying to make a departure from his HBO Tony Soprano image, succeeds in his sleazy role as the department store owner having an affair with Billy Bob's wife. This is revealed to us when both married couples are having dinner at Ed and Doris's home and Doris and Big Dave pick up on each other's jibes, in a very intimate fashion. Ed tells us in his voice-over how sure he is of their affair, but keeps on smoking!

What makes *The Man Who Wasn't There* so special as a revival of film noir is that, as in classic film noir, the twists and turns of the plot are the results of ironic turns of fate. And every character is caught up in a series of events that trap them and lead them to the gallows, rightly or wrongly. The only problem with *The Man Who Wasn't There* is its length. Most 1940s noir films are short films—some seventy to ninety minutes, shot in a tight black-and-white style that was indispensable to the story and part of the backgrounding. The Coen brothers have opted to use a luxurious 116 minutes to spin a ninety-minute tale of deceit and murder. Their black-and-white images seem too carefully crafted, too artsy, too pretty; and the pace is slowed by too many *longeurs* (moments of the camera deliberately dwelling), repetitive voice-overs, and a wandering script that could have been tightened for its own good. The Coen brothers' film is a small story exaggerated with noir style, taking far too much time to unravel. Films noirs stories of the 1940s and 1950s are executed at a rapid-fire pace on the screen; the noir style and cleverness of the plot were able to seep into the background, and moviegoers did not have to dwell on the details of plot or be overwhelmed by the artfulness of the style. The filmmaking then was more clever, sharper, and faster. If one must fault the Coen brothers in their reinvention of the noir in this film, it is for their indulgences in the script's length and excesses in photography. Yet, although the film may move slowly, credit Roger Deakins, the director of photography, because there is something interesting to watch in every artistic frame of *The Man Who Wasn't There*.

26. VANILLA SKY**** (2001)
135 minutes, Color

Director: Cameron Crowe.
Producers: Cameron Crowe, Tom Cruise, Paula Wagner.
Screenplay: Cameron Crowe, based on the screenplay *Abre los ojos* by Alejandro Amenábar and Mateo Gil.
Photography: John Toll.
Music: Nancy Wilson.
Editing: Joe Hutshing, Mark Livolsi.
Stars: Tom Cruise, Penélope Cruz, Cameron Diaz, Kurt Russell, Jason Lee.
CinemaScope. Paramount. VHS & DVD: Paramount.

Here is the remake of a sci-fi neo-noir 1997 Spanish film titled *Abre los ojos* (*Open Your Eyes*), directed by Alejandro Amenábar and starring Eduardo Noriega and Penélope Cruz. *Vanilla Sky* fits perfectly into our neo-noir category for the new millennium; it has a doomed hero, a femme fatale, and a twisty plot line whereby the hero does not get the money or the dame and walks away into a high-tech oblivion.

The film stars Tom Cruise as David Aames, the thirty-three-year-old wealthy son of deceased parents who runs a New York City publishing empire. David is a man who has *everything*—a terrific Manhattan apartment and a gorgeous lover, Julie Gianni (sharply played by blonde and beautiful Cameron Diaz), who will have sex with him anytime, anywhere (the truly fatal woman). Then he locks eyes with Sofia Serrano (Penélope Cruz), a Madridian beauty who teaches David the real meaning of love. Before an affair between the latter couple is consummated, Julie spirals into a whirlwind of rage. She offers to drive David home, but instead crashes her car, leaping an overpass near Riverside Park, killing herself and almost killing her lover, who is badly disfigured. David is forced to wear a mask to hide his scars and twisted flesh before he undergoes plastic surgery to restore his former good looks and reclaim the love of Sofia.

Here is where the plot of *Vanilla Sky* (named after the sky in a Monet painting) becomes a mind-bending noir thriller. Cameron Crowe, the director, has made a disturbing, exquisitely filmed sci-fi noir that has a frenetic storytelling pace and a unique blend of flashback sequences that serve as explorations of our own psyche. The original Spanish film is equally surreal in its conclusion, but it is cooler and more ambiguous than the U.S. version. Crowe adds some clarity and warmth to his version of *Open Your Eyes*. In it, David must finally decide—after we learn about his "splice"—whether to continue facing the trials and tribulations of a concrete life as a disfigured young man or retreat into a virtual-reality dreamscape with his good looks restored and the love of a beautiful woman (Sofia Serrano), who may or may not really exist.

In both films, David dreams he is walking alone in an absolutely deserted cityscape (downtown Madrid or Manhattan's Broadway); he is awakened by the impersonal voice of his alarm clock—*abre los ojos*; "open your eyes." We watch David's life spiral out of control as he is accused of Sofia's "murder" at one point and then learns about the "splice": he paid a futuristic cryogenic corporation to open his eyes, after his first dissolute life was over, and reawaken him into a second, paradisiacal, surreal life of wish fulfillment and love with a woman who is a computer creation. In both films, David elects to disregard his virtual-reality choice and plunges into a suicide dive.

Tom Cruise gives his best performance since *Born on the Fourth of July* (1989) in this surreal, sci-fi thriller/neo-noir. The film frustrates the viewer but has a haunting, lingering quality, with its twisty, deliciously exquisite plot turns. We also have Kurt Russell (out of his depth here) as a psychiatrist, supposedly helping Cruise and the audience steer through the possible or impossible plot consequences of Sofia Serrano's "murder."

The director, Cameron Crowe—like his predecessor, Alejandro Amenábar—leads us down many cul-de-sacs with Cruise narrating, until he finally opens his eyes, and we, the audience finally *see*! Two viewings are essential to discover whether David's life is real or a dream life he wants to pursue. *Vanilla Sky* is an ambitious, multifaceted film that crosses many genres and styles—horror, mystery, sci-fi thriller, and definitely noir. Its carefully constructed screenplay echoes some lines in Calderon de la Barca's famous Renaissance play *La vida es sueño*. "What is life? A dream, a frenzy . . . and even dreams are dreams."

27. BLOOD WORK*** (2002)
110 Minutes, Color

Director: Clint Eastwood.
Producer: Clint Eastwood.
Screenplay: Brian Helgeland, based on the novel by Michael Connelly.
Photography: Tom Stern.
Music: Lennie Niehaus.
Editing: Joel Cox.
Stars: Clint Eastwood, Jeff Daniels, Anjelica Huston, Wanda De Jesus.
CinemaScope. Malpaso/Warner Bros. VHS & DVD: Warner Bros.

Clint Eastwood is both star and director in this new noir revival of the serial killer theme. Screenwriter Brian Helgeland (who translated James Ellroy's *L.A. Confidential* from an almost intractable novel into an excellent screenplay in 1997) worked from a novel by Michael Connelly, which has a clever plot that is too coincidental for its own good. Eastwood plays Terry McCaleb, a cop who is forced off his last case because of a heart attack he suffers while chasing a serial murderer called the "Code Killer" down the streets of Los Angeles. He is lucky enough to receive a heart transplant, recovers from the surgery, and retires from the police force. Eastwood's portrait of McCaleb is Dirty Harry thirty-plus years down the road, although he has no laconic one-liners in this film and is also softer, gentler, and constantly aware of his mortality since the transplant operation. His doctor (played by Anjelica Huston) warns him not to go out on any more cases, especially in hot pursuit of the murderer of the woman who, coincidentally, was the organ donor for his new heart. Graciela Rivers (played effectively by Wanda De Jesus) identifies herself as the sister of his donor and asks Terry to catch her sister's murderer. Terry is moved by her plight and risks his life in this police procedural film which is tempered by a growing relationship between Terry and Graciela that ultimately turns to love.

Not too far into the film, Terry realizes it was the Code Killer who murdered Graciela's sister so that Terry could be the recipient of her heart. Apparently, the Code Killer had previous knowledge of their identical blood types and wanted to prolong Terry's life so that Terry and he could continue their cat-and-mouse chase. The killer is fond of leaving notes—like "Catch me McCaleb"—and Terry finally realizes his dockside pal Buddy Noone (an unfortunately miscast and unconvincing Jeff Daniels) is the murderer. At one point, Terry hires Buddy to drive him around during the investigation. Terry's donor's little son (now living with his aunt) realizes the phone number given

by the serial killer has no number one in it, and Buddy's last name is Noone—
"no one." Terry then confronts the latter at the dock. (Truthfully, this bit of
coincidental puzzle solving is an artifice that is unforgivable, especially since
it is so easy to see that the gofer and sidekick role of Buddy is too small for an
actor of Jeff Daniels's caliber. Viewers are likely to guess early on that he has
something to do with the serial murderer.)

Of course, Buddy Noone has one last card to play when Terry discovers his
identity. He has kidnapped Terry's new lover, Graciela, and her nephew, se-
questering them on a partially sunken freighter off the Los Angeles coast.
Terry forces Buddy to release them, but the latter eludes Terry until a final
shoot-out, in which Terry finally gets his man.

The title *Blood Work* appropriately sums up this well-crafted, back-to-
basics thriller about the hunt for a serial killer. The film's only defect is Jeff
Daniels, serving as comic relief throughout most of his screen time, until his
duplicity is revealed. He does not have the strength of character to make this
film the riveting neo-noir it could have been. Clint Eastwood's Terry is not a
reprise of Harry Callahan of the 1970s; he is a softer, caring person whose
tenderness exposes his vulnerability. That he is able to pull off the final chase
scene and murder the Code Killer is a bit too Hollywood and contrived.
Blood Work is a solid, classy, professional piece of filmmaking that builds some
tension but drops the ball early because of too many plot contrivances and
an unconvincing villain. Its plot hearkens back to film noir, but its soft-core
and minor forays into tense situations make it a marginal new noir. There is
not one gritty, hard, or unredeeming moment in the entire film—which is
just what this critic was hoping for.

Clint Eastwood would have been smarter to reprise his Dirty Harry character or use a younger, tougher actor in a tighter script that does not wallow
in sentimentality. *Blood Work* is definitely a marginal neo-noir that is mildly
entertaining.

28. INSOMNIA (2002)
116 minutes, Color

Director: Christopher Nolan.
Producers: Broderick Johnson, Paul Junger Witt, Andrew A. Kosove.
Screenplay: Hillary Seitz, based on a 1997 Norwegian film.
Photography: Wally Pfister.
Music: David Julyan.
Editing: Dody Dorn.
Stars: Al Pacino, Robin Williams, Hilary Swank, Martin Donovan.
CinemaScope. Warner Bros. VHS & DVD: Warners.

Insomnia is a remake of a 1997 Norwegian film noir with the same title, directed by Erik Skjoldbjaerg, in color, with Stellan Skarsgård playing the leading role. Surprisingly, it took only five years to appear as an American remake in color and CinemaScope, starring Al Pacino. Unlike *Blood Work*, which is set in Los Angeles, this film is set in *Alaska* (!), where (as in Norway) the summer sun does not set. And unlike most noir mysteries, which take place in the dark, this one is viewed in perpetual light. No, it is not a "film blanc," but a psychological game of wits between an experienced American detective, who brings his own dark impulses to a crime scene, and an equally dark serial killer. The killer's propensity is to bathe and manicure his victims after he abuses them sexually and murders them. The American version uses the original 1997 script but goes on for 118 minutes, compared to the original's ninety-seven minutes.

Third-time director Christopher Nolan is at the helm for his first major Hollywood production and does extremely well, especially in casting Al Pacino as Will Dormer, a Los Angeles detective who arrives with Martin Donovan (playing Hap Eckhart) in the small town of Nightmute, Alaska, in a twin-engine seaplane. They are greeted by Hilary Swank (playing detective Ellie Burr), who knows Dormer's reputation. She even did a term paper on Dormer's investigative techniques while at the police academy. Dormer is unable to sleep (hence the film's title), fearful that his partner, Eckhart, will go to internal affairs back in Los Angeles and reveal some irregularities in previous investigations and arrests that would result in Dormer's ouster. Dormer has nowhere to hide, not even in his dreams, because he suffers from insomnia.

Dormer and Eckhart devise a scheme to trap the murderer by releasing some false information on local television about the victim's recovered knapsack, which may hold the key to the murderer's identity. At a stakeout, the murderer shows up to retrieve the missing knapsack (it's Robin Williams as

Walter Finch, a clear-eyed, logical killer). What Dormer does not know is that there is another exit to the beach house where the stakeout takes place, through which Finch easily escapes. Following him on the fog-laden beach, Dormer sees a figure and fires his pistol, thinking it is Finch. It turns out to be Eckhart, who, before dying, accuses Dormer of murdering him to stop him from testifying in Los Angeles. Finch is hiding nearby; he hears this conversation and flees. Dormer sees the opportunity to blame Finch for his partner's murder and tampers with the evidence to throw suspicion on Finch. But since Finch knows the truth, he believes he has some power over Dormer and can make a deal.

Dormer's insomnia prevents him from thinking clearly and correctly; he is almost manipulated by Finch until a final shoot-out in which Finch is dispatched and Dormer finally admits the truth about the accidental shooting of his partner. Dormer boards a plane for Los Angeles, and we see the CinemaScope camera panning over the beautiful barren wastelands of jagged mountains and broken ice floes of Alaska (and British Columbia), where the film was actually made. Dormer will finally get some real sleep, as he faces the truth of Eckhart's shooting and probably the end of his career when he returns home.

The director added to the original screenplay some thrilling chase scenes, in one of which the leading actors run across logs rolling down a river, with Dormer caught underwater—or is it his dream of guilt that we see on-screen? Al Pacino looks correctly haggard throughout the film. But what makes this new noir *Insomnia* so exciting is the amoral character of Dormer, a supposedly brilliant investigator who is willing to have this police procedural turned in on itself as he juggles the evidence of Eckhart's accidental death while coming to terms with his own moral choices. So much of Pacino's wonderful acting concerns the mind of the character. To watch the morally straight character of Dormer warp into a villain is quite remarkable. (Stellan Skarsgård was even more remarkable in this transition in the 1997 original version.) This new *Insomnia* is beautifully shot, well acted, and suspenseful; it revives the noir style with great élan.

One last note on Christopher Nolan, the director. He is known for two earlier noirs, *Following* (1998) and *Memento* (2000). I deliberately chose not to review *Following*, despite the director's great talent in the noir arena of style. *Following*, Nolan's debut film, was shot in London with many unknown British actors and has a small, but interesting, premise—a man deliberately chooses a different person each day, intrudes on that person's life, and suffers the consequences. It was critically received with mixed reviews. *Memento* is reviewed above.

With the remake of *Insomnia*, I believe Christopher Nolan has come of age and full circle. He began with a small idea in *Following*, moved on to experimentation and fractured noir storytelling in *Memento*, and finally achieved, with *Insomnia*, a strong atmospheric film, linear and straightforward. In *Insomnia* the director has a lot of room in a far-northern location to solve the big-city complexities of a Los Angeles detective; in a terrain where there is perpetual light, there are clear choices to make. No tidy package, this film is an artful and expert foray into big-budget Hollywood production values, top talented actors, and story lines with psychological reverberations that have an entertaining resolution and linger in the mind a long while. *Insomnia* also reminds me of a black-and-white 1951 RKO Radio film directed by Nicholas Ray called *On Dangerous Ground*, starring Robert Ryan, a city detective who brutalizes his urban quarries and is sent to another state to track down the killer of a young girl in a bucolic setting. Ida Lupino plays the blind, good woman, sister of the murderer, who humanizes Ryan at the conclusion. We will await Nolan's next new noir film with anticipation and see where the journey leads us.

29. OUT OF TIME** (2003)
106 minutes, Color

Director: Carl Franklin.
Producers: Stokely Chaffin, Neal H. Moritz.
Screenplay: Dave Collard.
Photography: Theo Van de Sande.
Music: Graeme Revell.
Editing: Carole Kravetz.
Stars: Denzel Washington, Eva Mendes, Sanaa Lathan, Dean Cain.
CinemaScope. MGM. VHS & DVD: MGM.

After his award-winning role as a bad cop in *Training Day*, in *Out of Time* Denzel Washington plays a small-town Florida police chief, Matt Lee Whitaker, who is sort of good. He steals seven hundred thousand dollars in seized drug money to pay for experimental cancer therapy for his mistress, played by Sanaa Lathan. She supposedly dies with her husband (an extraordinary role played by Dean Cain) in a suspicious house fire; Matt is named as the beneficiary of her insurance policy; *and* the cache of money disappears when it is due to be handed over to FBI authorities the following day. Denzel investigates the case to clear himself of any impending charges of theft and suspected murder. To complicate the case, his estranged wife, played by Cuban-born actress Eva Mendes, is investigating the same double homicide by fire, while Denzel is trying to duck witnesses who saw him at the scene just before the fire.

This film is no reprise of Washington's stellar performance as Easy Rawlins in *Devil in a Blue Dress*, although this film was also directed by Carl Franklin. Franklin evokes, in almost every scene, the sweaty, humid atmosphere of southern Florida, and he creates some mildly suspenseful situations that our star seems to wriggle out of, somewhat undeservedly. This is definitely a neo-noir film that has reverberations of John Farrow's *The Big Clock* and Roger Donaldson's *No Way Out*. *Out of Time* is a plot-driven vehicle for its star-powered hero, who ultimately solves the crime and reunites with his ex-wife but is not a worthy character. In fact, you don't care a twit about most of the shallow characters in this noir film, because it is ultimately predictable, somewhat boring, sleazy, and even empty. Its star, who always seems to be on the edge, leads us into a phony world of crisscrosses and double crosses under the Florida sun, but without real tension or sexual electricity. When we discover his ex-mistress and her detective husband are alive and perpetuating this scam for the seized drug money, making Washington the patsy, we could not care less. After 105 minutes, this critic was relieved that the actors were really "out of time" to bore us further with an unjustifiable happy ending in this totally synthetic neo-noir thriller.

30. IN THE CUT**** (2003)
118 minutes, Color

Director: Jane Campion.
Producers: Nicole Kidman, Laurie Parker.
Screenplay: Jane Campion, Susanna Moore, based upon Susanna Moore's novel.
Photography: Dion Beebe.
Music: Hilmar Orne.
Editing: Alexandre de Franceschi.
Stars: Meg Ryan, Mark Ruffalo, Jennifer Jason Leigh.
CinemaScope. Screen-Gems/Pathé. VHS & DVD: Pathé.

Jane Campion, the illustrious New Zealand director of *The Piano* and *Portrait of a Lady*, made her first film in New York City with *In the Cut*, which might be called an East Village new noir. Meg Ryan stars as a high school English teacher searching for love and sex in all the wrong, sleazy places (compare Diane Keaton's role in *Looking for Mr. Goodbar*). She becomes enmeshed with a detective (wonderfully played by Mark Ruffalo) who is on the hunt for a serial killer who "disarticulates" (substitute "beheads") his victims after forcing an engagement ring on their left hand and violating them sexually. The real star of the film is the director of photography, Dion Beebe, whose jumpy camera (very reminiscent of that in the film *Se7en*) shows in detail the gritty realities of the bars, apartments, cramped streets, and basements of Soho, Greenwich Village, and lower Manhattan. The darkness of the photography parallels the moral sleaziness of the characters as well as the actions of the serial killer.

Meg Ryan gets naked and frisky in this film, as does Mark Ruffalo, and they talk a lot about sex, fellatio, and the "sensitivity of the cock." It seems Ruffalo has a tattoo of a spade and a number on his left hand, as does his detective partner, wonderfully played by Nick Damici, who turns out to be the real killer. Having handcuffed Ruffalo to a steam pipe in her apartment, Ryan goes off with Damici and, after seeing *his* tattoo, realizes she is with the serial killer. She finds a gun in Ruffalo's suit jacket, which she had hurriedly thrown over her dress before leaving her apartment. Although we don't actually hear the shot, we watch from a helicopter shot Damici laying on top of Ryan, with a bloodspot widening on the center of his back. In her bloody clothes, Ryan is somehow able to hitchhike back to her apartment, where she reunites with the handcuffed Ruffalo in probably one of the most contrived and bizarre noir endings ever concocted.

Two excellent actors who fill the spaces between the leading players and the investigation are Jennifer Jason Leigh and Kevin Bacon. Leigh plays the boozy half-sister of Ryan, who lives above the "Baby Doll Lounge," and her transient, prurient lifestyle prefigures her fate as one of the serial killer's victims. Bacon is equally good as Ryan's ex-lover, a disenfranchised doctor; unshaven, wearing hospital scrubs and a baseball cap, he is followed by a ratty-looking dog and is always shouting obscenities when things don't go his way with Ryan.

Although this critic would not venture a guess as to the significance of the title of this film, nevertheless, one can safely assert that the director, Campion, has followed the rules for making a noir thriller. She has successfully explored East Village paranoia and the shadowy parts of New York life in this malevolent and occult mystery with a sense of danger in every scene. This world of New York will ultimately confuse and confound you, even in bright sunlight. Although the film may deal with big themes like sex, death, language, and ultimately love, it is still basically a noir about accusing the wrong man, with a deliberately screwy ending. Ryan's mistaken identity of Ruffalo as the killer she supposedly comes to love is the thread on which the entire narrative hangs. What saves *In the Cut* from being a pedestrian thriller is the erotic psychodrama between the leading actors and those wonderful photographic images that always summon up feelings of edginess and danger, even in bright sunlight. One wonders what the next American film will be from this very talented New Zealand director.

31. MYSTIC RIVER**** (2003)
137 minutes, Color

Director: Clint Eastwood.
Producers: Clint Eastwood, Judie Hoyt, Robert Lorenz.
Screenplay: Brian Helgeland, based on Dennis Lehane's novel.
Photography: Tom Stern.
Music: Clint Eastwood.
Editing: Joel Cox.
Stars: Sean Penn, Tim Robbins, Marcia Gay Harden, Kevin Bacon, Laurence Fishburne, Laura Linney.
CinemaScope. Warner Bros. VHS & DVD: Warner Bros.

Probably the best neo-noir film of 2003, in which darkness pervades each character's motivations, *Mystic River* is a crime thriller, based on Dennis Lehane's novel, scripted by Brian Helgeland (*L.A. Confidential*), and directed by Clint Eastwood. It begins in a Boston Irish neighborhood in the mid-1970s, when three friends are playing stickball and one of them, the Tim Robbins character, is abducted by a phony policeman and priest who abuse him. The film cuts to the present, and we learn Robbins is married to Marcia Gay Harden and has a son of his own but is tormented by the memories of his abuse, his escape ("the boy who escaped from wolves"), and his loss of innocence. His friends, Sean Penn and Kevin Bacon, have grown up differently even though they live in the same neighborhood. Penn is an ex-convict who runs a local grocery store with his children by his second wife, marvelously played by Laura Linney, and Kevin Bacon is a cop on the local police force who lives alone, suffering because he caused the estrangement of his wife and child.

All three childhood friends are drawn together when Penn's daughter Katie (played by Emmy Rossum) is found murdered in a nearby park. Gay Harden suspects her husband, Tim Robbins, of the crime and reveals that he came home on the evening of the murder with his clothes covered in blood. Penn seeks vengeance and, with members of his local gang, stabs Robbins to death, pushing his body into the darkness and depths of the Mystic River.

In a subplot, we learn Katie was going to run away with her boyfriend, Brendan (played by Thomas Guiry), the following day and was celebrating her departure at a local bar the evening of her murder with two girlfriends. Penn cautioned his daughter to have nothing to do with Brendan, because it was Brendan's father who initially caused Penn to be jailed. (Penn admits to murdering Brendan's father later on in the film, a murder undiscovered by the police, and also admits to sending Brendan's mother monthly five-hundred-dollar checks in the name of Brendan's father, who is supposedly alive and in Brooklyn.)

In this densely woven narrative, we finally learn the real truth. It was one of Brendan's brothers, a mute, who killed Katie because he did not want Brendan to desert him and the family. Bacon, the cop, informs Penn of the news, and the latter realizes his mistake in killing Robbins after getting the latter to admit to his daughter's murder. When Gay Harden realizes she mistakenly caused her husband's death, she must live alone with her betrayal. But Laura Linney, Penn's wife, supports her husband's ruthlessness, which passes for justice in the world. She sees nothing wrong in Penn's dispatch of the Robbins character, who is revealed to have killed a number of pederasts in the Boston area and gotten away with the crimes. In fact, she sees her husband as a leader in the neighborhood, and supports the notion that the tragedy of their daughter's death is the source of their grief, loyalty, and even love. Penn says at one point, "We bury our sins and wash them clean."

The film then cuts to an Independence Day parade, and we see the Gay Harden character watching her son marching proudly. (She is probably receiving monthly five-hundred-dollar checks from Penn.) Linney, fiercely devoted to Penn, stands proudly at the parade with her husband. And Kevin Bacon's estranged wife and child have finally returned to Boston, which gives the film a bittersweet ending.

It is hard to think of a darker, more memorable film, filled with shadows and impending danger. Its labyrinthine plot, stemming from a truly excellent crime novel, evolves through many different characters with multifaceted motives. In fact, every character seems to be harboring a dark secret or an ulterior motive and a great intensity of feeling that cannot be quelled. Even murder and child molestation cannot be rectified by the forces of law and order; personal vengeance, vigilantism undiscovered, is the rule. The emotional power of these characters will resonate with the viewer long after the end of the film.

As the camera swoops down in its final evening shot into the Mystic River and the end titles come up on the screen, you realize you have been through a terrific experience—wonderful ensemble acting, especially Sean Penn's performance as the grief-stricken father—but you feel no catharsis, instead a bit beaten up by the conclusion, and the darkness stays with you. You have seen one of the best new noirs of the millennium.

32. COLLATERAL**** (2004)
119 minutes, Color

Director: Michael Mann.
Producers: Michael Mann, Judy Richardson.
Screenplay: Stuart Beattie.
Photography: Dion Beebe, Paul Cameron.
Music: James Newton Howard.
Editing: Jim Miller, Paul Rubell.
Stars: Tom Cruise, Jamie Foxx, Mark Ruffalo, Peter Berg, Jada Pinkett Smith.
CinemaScope. 20th Century Fox. VHS & DVD: Fox.

Collateral is the best neo-noir to be released in 2004, the most beautifully photographed (using the new digital process), and the most impressive directorial effort of Michael Mann to date. It stars Tom Cruise, playing against type, as a gray-haired hit man working for a Colombian drug cartel headed by Spanish actor Javier Bardem (who is seen briefly in one nightclub scene.)

Cruise, as Vincent, arrives in Los Angeles, dressed in a gray suit and carrying an attaché case, his gray beard in need of a trim. He is picked up by a black cab driver, Max (wonderfully played by Jamie Foxx); the latter has just returned from downtown Los Angeles, where he drove his previous fare, Annie (played by Jada Pinkett Smith), to her office. She is coincidentally a district attorney preparing her case against the Colombian drug lords for presentation the next morning and is working at her office on the evening of Vincent's arrival. Little does she know she is number five on Vincent's hit list. The plot turns on Vincent's taking Max hostage so he can carry out his serial murders and Max's realization that he must get away from Vincent and warn the district attorney, on whom he has a slight romantic crush.

When Vincent first enters Max's cab, they strike up an amiable conversation. Vincent offers Max six hundred dollars to drive him to several destinations, and the latter accepts the cash, since he would like to be an independent limousine owner and is saving his money to fulfill this dream. But after Max drops Vincent off at his first stop, a man's body comes hurtling out of a fourth-story window, riddled with bullets, and lands on top of Max's cab, slightly breaking his windshield. Helping Vincent take the body off the top of his cab, Max realizes he is in big trouble. In fact, most of the film consists of a series of confrontations between the two men, each trying to accomplish his own goals.

Max is now a victim of Vincent, kidnapped, helping him to accomplish his murderous agenda. He must try to get away, but Vincent ties him to the steering wheel while he commits yet another murder, this of a Latino family man in his upscale apartment. Max tries to get a group of passers-by to free him; they, in turn, steal Max's cash and Vincent's attaché case. But Vincent surprises them and kills another two men, warning Max not to seek help or he'll blow him away. Realizing he will have to take Max with him wherever he goes, Vincent, with Max, enters an intimate Los Angeles jazz club and stays after hours, complimenting a musician on his playing while they share drinks; then Vincent shoots the musician dead at the table.

Meanwhile, a collection of bodies is piling up at the Los Angeles morgue, and three detectives, especially Mark Ruffalo, notice a connection to the Colombian cartel. He realizes another of the witnesses in the next day's trial is at a huge nightclub across town and enlists the aid of the FBI and local detectives, played by Peter Berg and Bruce McGill. Vincent and Max enter the nightclub, with the police hot on Vincent's trail. But Vincent is a dedicated professional and never misses his mark! In a scene loaded with dancers, multiple orchestras, and food and drinks being served, Vincent scores again, also killing one of the detectives (Ruffalo), and escapes with Max in his taxi. Max reacts so violently to Vincent's murders that he tosses Vincent's attaché case out of the cab onto the highway below as they drive deeper into Los Angeles.

There are wonderful helicopter shots that trace the cab's journey from one destination to another. What Vincent and Max don't know is that the FBI is using high-tech cameras to trace their trajectory and have finally identified Max as the driver of the damaged cab. Vincent is enraged that Max has thrown the attaché case out the window; he makes Max go into another club and demand from the Colombian drug kingpin a computer copy of his hit list to complete his job. This is an improbable scene, as is Vincent and Max's visiting the latter's mother at a local hospital to give the appearance of normalcy to Max's activities. Vincent gets the address of his last target from the drug kingpin, and Max realizes it is Annie, the district attorney. This time, Max takes Vincent on a wild ride on Los Angeles streets, deliberately crashing his cab. Both men survive, and Vincent crawls out from the overturned cab, relentlessly pursuing his final target. Max tries to warn Annie (he has her business card) using a dying cell phone. He succeeds and runs to her building, taking her outside with Vincent in hot pursuit.

The conclusion takes place aboard the Los Angeles metro. Max winds up shooting Vincent dead after a long and terrifying chase, leaving Vincent aboard the train as he and Annie leave the scene hand in hand. This is perhaps an improbable ending, but nevertheless *Collateral* is an exciting, flawlessly photographed new noir film. Gunplay, violence, and chase scenes galore define the atmosphere of the film. But the lead actors save the day because they really involve us in their struggles and play well off each other's roles.

The screenplay is also compelling because, in this unconventional buddy story, the protagonists don't bond as the action wears on and the weaknesses and strengths of each character are exposed. Vincent remains the same cold-blooded killer at the end of the film as he was at the beginning. It is in Max's character that we experience a change—he moves from being a dreamer to being a realist. His performance involves the viewers completely. His courageous acts and development as a man, leavened with Michael Mann's technical expertise, save this film from being just another new noir action thriller. Mann is especially good using tracking shots throughout the nightclub scenes. His camera work is fluid. The film has a luxurious sense of movement and depth, and it is a terrifically pleasurable experience to watch it again and again.

Afterword

The new noir style continues to be a favorite of film directors, actors, and audiences alike. A revival of gangster themes, caper films, remakes of new noirs of the 1990s involving police procedurals or the tracking down of serial killers, sci-fi noirs, remakes of 1940s noirs updated to the twenty-first century, and, finally, the ultimate sendup of the "original" film noir style, refashioned with the latest projection techniques—graphic novels in black and white!

I have just seen a preview of *Sin City*, a Frank Miller graphic novel adapted to film, directed by Miller and Robert Rodriguez. The film stars Bruce Willis, Josh Hartnett, Maria Bello, Jaime King, and Mickey Rourke. Mickey Rourke plays Marv, who is looking for the person who killed his one true love, Goldie (played by Jaime King), as he "trawls the darkest areas of Sin City."

Noir is taking a wholly different stylistic turn this year, reviving pulp conventions. But whether we call this new film a "new noir" or a "nouveau noir" or a "neo-noir," the style will continue moving forward into the new millennium; it will never surrender or be eclipsed but will go on relentlessly. To reiterate, as long as there are men and women involved in crime and seduction, films noirs and their new spin-offs will endure.

~

An "A to Z" Rated Filmography of Neo-Noir Films (1960–2004)

The following is a select but fairly inclusive neo-noir filmography from 1960 to 2004. The film title, year of release, and director's name are followed by annotations **in bold** to offer some sense of the style, plot, or subgenre of each film. A comprehensive listing of credits, actors, and plot outlines may be obtained by visiting the Internet Movie Database (www.imdb.com). Also, a series of useful film reference books is cited in the select bibliography of this volume. As with the films discussed previously, starred ratings following each title signify the worth of the film as follows:

**** Outstanding
*** Excellent
** Good
* Poor
No stars: for the die-hard noir fan only

The Accused*** (1988) Jonathan Kaplan **Boston gang rape / feminist noir**
Across 110th Street** (1972) Barry Shear **Black gangster noir**
After Dark, My Sweet*** (1990) James Foley **Retarded boxer / femme fatale / heist**
After Hours*** (1985) Martin Scorsese **Surreal screwball / comedy noir**
Against All Odds*** (1984) Taylor Hackford **Color remake of *Out of the Past* / double cross / femme fatale / California and Cancun locales**

Albino Alligator** (1997) Kevin Spacey **Cop murder / hostages / escape**

Alligator Eyes* (1990) John Feldman **Hitchhiker / femme fatale**

All the President's Men*** (1976) Alan J. Pakula **True political noir / newspaper ambience**

Along Came a Spider*** (2001) Lee Tamahori **Criminal profiler tracks kidnappers in Washington DC**

Amateur** (1994) Hal Hartley **Porn star / criminal amnesiac**

The American Friend*** (1977) Wim Wenders **Gangster / Mafia / assassin**

American Gigolo** (1980) Paul Schrader **Homme fatale / gigolo / murder**

American Me*** (1992) Edward James Olmos **Chicano prison film / drugs**

Angel Heart** (1987) Alan Parker **Devil incarnate / New Orleans murder**

Another 48 Hours** (1990) Walter Hill **Cop thriller / car chases**

Apartment Zero** (1988) Martin Donovan **Homoerotic / serial murder noir**

Apology* (1986) Robert Bierman **Psychotic killer / stalker / New York City noir**

Atlantic City*** (1981) Louis Malle **Mafia heist / femme fatale / nudity**

Auto Focus*** (2002) Paul Schrader **Biopic of TV star Bob Crane / sexploits**

Backfire* (1987) Gilbert Cates **Noir triangle / sex / double cross / murder**

Backstreet Jane* (1989) Ronnie Cramer **Femme thief or extortionist?**

Bad Boys** (1983) Rick Rosenthal **Teen prison drama**

Bad Boys** (1995) Michael Bay **Black cop buddies / spoof / femmes fatales**

Bad Company** (1995) Damian Harris **Illegal criminal organization**

The Badge* (2002) Robby Henson **Sheriff looks into murder of transsexual / political implications**

Bad Influence*** (1990) Curtis Hanson **Domineering criminal / murder**

Badlands*** (1973) Terrence Malick **Real fugitive couple / serial killers**

Bad Lieutenant** (1992) Abel Ferrara **New York City bad cop / nudity / rape / crime**

Barton Fink**** (1991) Joel Coen **Retro 1940s Hollywood noir**

Basic Instinct** (1992) Paul Verhoeven **Ice pick murder / sexual flashing**

Batman** (1989) Tim Burton **Comic book noir**

Batman and Robin** (1997) Joel Schumacher **Comic book noir reprise / camp**

Batman Forever** (1995) Joel Schumacher **Comic book reprise / less noir**

Batman Returns*** (1992) Tim Burton **Comic book noir / nightmarish sets**

Beautiful Creatures** (2000) Bill Eagles **Scottish comedy noir / corrupt detective**

The Bedroom Window** (1987) Curtis Hanson **Femme fatale / attack / revenge**

Best Laid Plans** (1997) Mike Barker **Flashbacks / townie teen thieves**

Best Seller*** (1987) John Flynn **Jaded cop and author/psychotic killer team**

Betrayal** (1974) Gordon Hessler **Psycho-thriller / murder for cash**

Betrayed** (1988) Costa-Gavras **FBI agent joins white supremacist group**

The Big Easy*** (1986) Jim McBride **New Orleans detective / drug wars**

The Big Fix** (1978) Jeremy Kagan **Jewish detective hunts protester**

The Big Lebowski*** (1998) Joel Coen **Detective tracks kidnapped wife**

The Big Sleep** (1978) Michael Winner **Colorful remake / drugs / murders**

The Big Squeeze** (1996) Marcus de Leon **Couple kill for husband's cash**

Big Trouble** (1986) John Cassavetes **Fraud scheme sends sons to college**

Bitter Moon*** (1992) Roman Polanski **Femme fatale / ménage à quatre cruise**

The Black Bird (1975) David Giler **Satiric spoof of *Maltese Falcon***

Black Eye (1974) Jack Arnold **Blaxploitation / detective / drugs**

Black Rain** (1989) Ridley Scott **New York City detectives in Japan / yakuza mob**

Black Sunday*** (1977) John Frankenheimer **Terrorist noir / bomb plot**

Black Widow** (1987) Bob Rafelson **Femme fatale serial killer / poisoner**

Blade Runner*** (1982) Ridley Scott **Sci-fi thriller / cops vs. androids**

The Blair Witch Project (1999) Daniel Myrick **Maryland disappearances / hoax neo-noir style**

Blast of Silence** (1961) Allen Baron **New York City / hired killer's life and death**

Blondes Have More Guns* (1995) George Merriweather **Spoof of *Basic Instinct* and *Lethal Weapon***

Blood and Wine** (1997) Bob Rafelson **Florida-set heist film**

Blood In, Blood Out** (1993) Taylor Hackford **Chicano crime / prison film**

Blow Out** (1981) Brian De Palma **Political conspiracy / U.S. senator killed**

Blue Desert (1992) Bradley Battersby **New York City rape victim / dangers in West**

Blue Steel** (1990) Katheryn Bigelow **Romance / female cop and serial killer**

Blue Velvet** (1986) David Lynch **Small town murder / masochism / violence**

Bodily Harm (1995) James Lemmo **Female detective / corrupt cop / murder**

Body and Soul (1981) George Bowers **Blaxploitation remake of 1947 film**

Body and Soul (1998) Sam Kass **Real-life pugilist in Garfield remake**

Body Chemistry (1990) Kristine Peterson **Extramarital affair / revenge**

Body Double** (1984) Brian De Palma **Voyeurism / pornography / murder**

The Bodyguard** (1992) Mick Jackson **FBI agent falls for singer femme fatale**

Body of Evidence (1993) Uli Edel **Sex as weapon / nudity / sadomasochism**

Body Parts (1991) Eric Red **Sci-fi / horror / arm transplant causes murder**

Boiling Point** (1993) James B. Harris **Retro 1940s noir / murder and manhunt**

Bonnie and Clyde**** (1967) Arthur Penn **Biopic / robbers / slow-motion murder**

The Border** (1982) Tony Richardson **Mexican immigration / corruption**

The Boston Strangler*** (1968) Richard Fleischer **Docu-noir / serial killer**

Bound*** (1996) Andy and Larry Wachowski **Lesbian heist of male mafiosi**

Boxing Helena** (1993) Jennifer Lynch **Sexual obsession / mutilation**

A Boy Called Hate (1995) Mitch Marcus **Road movie / fugitive couple**

Boyz N the Hood* (1991) John Singleton **Teenage crime in central Los Angeles**

Brainstorm* (1965) William Conrad **Love triangle leads to insanity**

Breakdown (1997) Jonathan Mostow **Kidnapping / murder / revenge**

Breathless*** (1983) Jim McBride **Colorful remake / petty car thief / nudity**

Bright Angel (1991) Michael Fields **Western road movie / jailbreak**

Bring Me the Head of Alfredo Garcia** (1974) Sam Peckinpah **Piano player turned bounty killer / Mexican locale**

Brown's Requiem** (1998) Jason Freeland **ex–Los Angeles cop / kidnapping / murder**

Bulletproof Heart*** (1994) Mark Malone **Hit man falls for socialite**

Bullitt*** (1968) Peter Yates **Rogue cop vs. criminals / San Francisco car chases**

Cafe Society*** (1997) Raymond de Felitta **Jelke heir runs call-girl ring / retro 1950s noir**

Call Me (1988) Sollace Mitchell **Woman on the run from organized crime**

Cape Fear*** (1962) J. Lee Thompson **Revenge noir / demented villain**

Cape Fear** (1991) Martin Scorsese **Color remake / revenge of psychopath**

Captives (1994) Angela Pope **British prison noir / love and revenge**

Carlito's Way** (1993) Brian De Palma **Fictional biopic of Puerto Rican gangster**

Casino** (1995) Martin Scorsese **Gangster's downfall in Las Vegas**

Cat Chaser* (1989) Abel Ferrara **Ex-soldier's affair with Dominican dictator's wife / from Elmore Leonard novel**

Catherine's Grove (1997) Rick King **PI tracks serial killer in Miami**

Caught** (1996) Robert M. Young **Drifter seduces Latina wife of Miami fish purveyor / family takes revenge**

Cellular** (2004) David R. Ellis **Kidnapped femme relies on cell phone for help**

Chandler* (1971) Paul Magwood **PI falls for mobster's wife / retro noir**

Charly Varrick*** (1973) Don Siegel **Bank robber steals from Mafia in New Mexico**

The Chase* (1966) Arthur Penn **Revenge drama / sheriff vs. convict / Texas**

The Cheap Detective* (1978) Robert Moore **Parody of *Maltese Falcon***

China Moon*** (1994) John Bailey **Cop kills banker for cash and femme fatale**

Circus (2000) Rob Walker **British noir / gambler takes over mob in Brighton**

City of Ghosts* (2002) Matt Dillon **Con man in Cambodia / insurance scam**

City of Industry** (1997) John Irvin **Heist / double cross / revenge / violence**

Clay Pigeons** (1998) David Dobkin **Serial killer / femme fatale / Montana**

Clockers* (1995) Spike Lee **Black drug peddlers in tenements vs. cops**

Cold around the Heart* (1998) John Ridley **Crime / road movie / infidelity**

Color Me Dead (1969) Eddie Davis **DOA remake / poisoned man tracks his murderer in Australia**

Colors* (1988) Dennis Hopper **Los Angeles police procedural / dark gang culture**

The Conversation*** (1974) Francis Ford Coppola **Furtive surveillance**

Coogan's Bluff** (1968) Don Siegel **Arizona cop tracks perp in New York City**

Cool Breeze (1994) Barry Pollack **Black remake of *Asphalt Jungle***

Cop** (1988) James B. Harris **Twisted detective tracks serial killer**

Cop Land** (1997) James Mangold **Internal affairs tracks New York cops in New Jersey**

*Copycat** (1995) Jon Amiel **Psychologist tracked by southern sociopath**

*The Cotton Club** (1984) Francis Ford Coppola **Retro gangster noir of 1920s**

*Crash** (1997) David Cronenberg **Flesh-to-metal contact leads to sex**

*Crimes and Misdemeanors*** (1989) Woody Allen **Hit man / no-guilt noir**

*Criminal Law*** (1988) Martin Campbell **Boston noir / serial rapist freed**

Crosscurrent (1971) Jerry Thorpe **Two San Francisco cops look for cable-car killer**

*Croupier*** (1997) Mike Hodges **British neo-noir / gambler loses money and dame**

*The Crow**** (1994) Alex Proyas **Revenge fantasy noir / Detroit locale**

*The Crow: City of Angels*** (1996) Tim Pope **Sequel / revenge / Los Angeles locale**

Crude Oasis (1995) Alex Graves **Moody suspenser / love and death in Kansas**

*Cruel Intentions*** (2001) Roger Kumble **Teen seduction / dark consequences**

*Cruising**** (1980) William Friedkin **Cop and New York City gays / serial-killer noir**

*Cutter's Way*** (1981) Ivan Passer **Male couple bonds to solve murder**

*Dance with a Stranger*** (1985) Mike Newell **British femme gangster hanged**

Dangerously Close (1986) John Stockwell **High school kids become neo-fascists**

Dark Blue (2002) Ron Shelton **Los Angeles corrupt cop changes tactics**

*Dark City**** (1998) Alex Proyas **Twenty-first-century sci-fi joins 1940s noir**

*The Dark Wind** (1992) Errol Morris **PI in Navajo territory / cultish / drugs**

*Darker Than Amber** (1973) Robert Clouse **Seedy Florida PI falls for dame**

*The Day of the Jackal**** (1973) Fred Zinnemann **Attempted murder of French general Charles De Gaulle by professional assassin**

*Dead Again*** (1991) Kenneth Branagh **Los Angeles dick delves into 1940s murder**

Dead Awake (2001) Mark S. Grenier **Sleepwalker witnesses murder**

*Dead-Bang*** (1989) John Frankenheimer **Cop rounds up neo-Nazi murderers**

*Dead Calm*** (1989) Philip Noyce **Couple on yacht pick up psycho killer**

*Dead Men Don't Wear Plaid**** (1982) Carl Reiner **Spoof of 1940s noir**

The Dead Pool** (1988) Buddy Van Horn **Dirty Harry as celebrity target**
Dead Presidents** (1995) Allen Hughes **Failed heist by black Vietnam vets**
Dead Silence (1990) Dan Petrie **FBI rescues deaf hostages from convicts**
Death Wish** (1974) Michael Winner **Husband turns vigilante after rape**
Death Wish 2** (1981) Michael Winner **Los Angeles vigilante after serial rapist**
Death Wish 3** (1985) Michael Winner **Vigilante on New York City subway**
Death Wish 4: The Crackdown** (1987) J. Lee Thompson **Vigilante in Los Angeles**
Death Wish 5: The Face of Death** (1993) Allen Goldstein **Vigilante in New York City garment district**
Deceived** (1991) Damian Harris **Pseudo-Hitchcock thriller / vanishing man**
Deceiver (1998) Jonas Pate **Prostitute murdered by lying playboy**
Deception** (1993) Graeme Clifford **Disappearing husband tracked by wife**
Deep Cover** (1992) Bill Duke **Undercover cop exposes Los Angeles drug lord**
Defenseless* (1991) Martin Campbell **Los Angeles attorney solves crime of lover's wife**
Delusion* (1991) Carl Colparet **Reno thief picks up dame / road movie**
Desperate Hours* (1990) Michael Cimino **Remake / criminal takes hostages**
Destiny Turns on the Radio (1995) Quentin Tarantino **Magical-realism noir at its worst / robber recovers loot and wife**
The Detective** (1968) Gordon Douglas **New York City cop hunts serial killer of gay men**
Detour** (1992) Wade Williams **Expanded color remake / fatalistic noir**
Devil in a Blue Dress*** (1995) Carl Franklin **Black PI / murder and politics in Los Angeles**
Diary of a Hitman* (1992) Roy London **Killer saves intended victim**
Dick Tracy** (1990) Warren Beatty **Retro 1930s comic strip noir**
Dillinger** (1973) John Milius **Biopic / retro 1930s gangster / color remake**
Dirty Money** (1972) Jean-Pierre Melville **Two heists / police pursue**
Disclosure** (1994) Barry Levinson **Sexual harassment neo-noir**
D.O.A.** (1988) Rocky Morton and Annabel Jankel **Poisoned professor tracks down murderer / trendy color remake of 1949 noir**

Dog Day Afternoon** (1975) Sidney Lumet **Brooklyn heist by gay man goes awry**

Donnie Brasco** (1997) Mike Newell **FBI infiltrates Mafia**

Dressed to Kill** (1980) Brian De Palma **Derivative psycho-serial killer neo-noir**

The Driver** (1978) Walter Hill **Jewel thief / car chases / minimalist noir**

The Drowning Pool* (1975) Stuart Rosenberg **PI / blackmail / New Orleans**

Drugstore Cowboy*** (1989) Gus Van Sant **Nonjudgmental noir / drug addicts**

8 Million Ways to Die** (1986) Hal Ashby **Ex-cop / drugs / murder / sex**

8 mm.** (1999) Joel Schumacher **PI investigates snuff films and porno**

El Mariachi** (1992) Robert Rodriguez **Chicano parody of Mexican noir**

The Enforcer** (1976) James Fargol **Dirty Harry hunts terrorists**

Equinox* (1993) Alan Rudolph **Futuristic gangster / romantic neo-noir**

Eve's Bayou** (1997) Kasi Lemmons **Noirish memories / adulterous father / black society / Louisiana 1962**

Exotica* (1994) Atom Egoyan **Nightclub ambience / lap dancing / voyeurism**

Experiment in Terror** (1962) Blake Edwards **Kidnapping and blackmail / FBI in San Francisco**

Exterior Night*** (1994) Mark Rappaport **Rear projection screens of 1940s films / high-definition television plates / new noir *and* retro techniques / love and death**

Eyes of Laura Mars* (1978) Irvin Kershner **Photographer predicts murders**

Eyewitness* (1981) Peter Yates **Janitor lies to femme reporter / murder**

Face Down (1997) Thom Eberhardt **Ex–New York City cop, best friend solve murder**

Face/Off*** (1997) John Woo **Stolen identities: ultraviolent sci-fi noir**

Fade to Black** (1980) Vernon Zimmerman **Killer adopts film baddie roles**

Fallen Angels** (1993); Pt. 2 (1995) Various directors **Six old and new noir short stories for HBO**

Falling Down** (1993) Joel Schumacher **Vigilante revenge fantasy in Los Angeles**

Farewell, My Lovely*** (1975) Dick Richards **Color remake / 1941 Los Angeles / Chandler / drugs / prostitution / nymphomania / gambling**

Fargo*** (1996) Joel Coen **Woman police chief investigates swindle / kidnapping**

Fatal Attraction*** (1987) Adrian Lyne **New York City husband strays / violent ending**

Fatal Instinct* (1991) John Dirlam **PI falls for femme while tracking murderer of real estate tycoon**

Fatal Instinct** (1993) Carl Reiner **Parody / sendup of noir tradition**

Fear** (1996) James Foley **Manipulative youth almost destroys family**

Fear City* (1984) Abel Ferrara **Psychopath kills Manhattan strippers**

Femme Fatale* (1991) Andre Guttfreund **Bride disappears / double life / Los Angeles**

Femme Fatale** (2002) Brian De Palma **Ten-million-dollar jewel heist / stolen identity**

52 Pick-Up** (1986) John Frankenheimer **Affair / blackmail / violence**

Final Analysis** (1992) Phil Joanau **Psychiatrist / patient relations sour**

Finder's Fee (2001) Jeff Probst **New York City man finds wallet with two-million-dollar winning lottery ticket**

Fingers** (1978) James Toback **Gang debt collector dreams: pianist future**

First Blood*** (1982) Ted Kotcheff **Revenge fantasy of ex–Vietnam killer**

The First Deadly Sin** (1980) Brian Hutton **Retired detective tracks killer**

First Degree (1995) Jeff Woolnough **Detective vs. the mob / love and murder**

A Flash of Green*** (1984) Victor Nunez **Reporter and lover in Florida land grab**

Flesh and Bone*** (1993) Steven Kloves **Rural Texas / son escapes dad's past**

Following**** (1998) Christopher Nolan **Brit's penchant leads to crime**

48 Hours** (1982) Walter Hill **Detective springs con to find murderer**

Frantic** (1988) Roman Polanski **Kidnapped wife / heroic husband searches Paris**

The French Connection II** (1974) John Frankenheimer **New York City detective tracks heroin ring in Marseilles in sequel**

The Friends of Eddie Coyle*** (1973) Peter Yates **Boston underworld / heists**

Frisk (1995) Todd Verow **Los Angeles sadomasochism scene / sex, murder fantasies**

From Dusk till Dawn (1996) Quentin Tarantino **Escaped cons / hostages / vampires**

The Fugitive** (1993) Andrew Davis **Con escapes / looks for wife's killer**

The Funeral** (1996) Abel Ferrara **Italian brothers solve Mafia murders**

Funeral in Berlin** (1966) Guy Hamilton **Espionage and Russian defectors**

The Game** (1997) David Fincher **Virtual reality traps victim in games**
Gang Related (1997) Jim Kouf **Homicide cops on the take from drug ring**
Gattaca** (1997) Andrew Niccol **Sci-fi noir / identity exchanges / murder**
The Gauntlet** (1977) Clint Eastwood **Cop finds femme fatale to testify**
Genuine Risk (1990) Kurt Voss **Femme seduces bodyguard of gangster lover**
The Getaway*** (1973) Walter Hill **Bank heist / amoral cops / car chases**
The Getaway (1994) Roger Donaldson **Bank heist / amoral cops / remake**
Get Carter*** (1971) Mike Hodges **British hood plots revenge for brother**
Get Carter (2000) Stephen Kay **Updated neo-noir remake / revenge plot**
Get Shorty** (1995) Barry Sonnenfeld **Miami hoods / Las Vegas debtors**
Ghost Dog** (2000) Jim Jarmusch **Black assassin / vengeance neo-noir**
The Gingerbread Man** (1998) Robert Altman **Savannah noir / femme fatale has dad committed by local lawyer**
The Girl Hunters* (1963) Roy Rowland **PI Mickey Spillane / Communist spies and femme fatale**
The Glass House** (2001) Daniel Sackheim **Stepparents fleece children**
Gleaming the Cube** (1989) Graeme Clifford **Teen solves brother's murder**
Glengarry Glen Ross**** (1992) James Foley **Sleazy salesmen compete for jobs**
Gloria** (1980) John Cassavetes **One woman against the mob / colorful**
The Godfather**** (1972) Francis Ford Coppola **Rise and fall of Mafia family / epic gangster trilogy**
The Godfather, Part II**** (1974) Francis Ford Coppola **Continuation: mafioso arrives around 1920**
The Godfather, Part III** (1990) Francis Ford Coppola **Corleone buys into papacy / trilogy ends**
Golden Gate** (1994) John Madden **Fed agent / Commie witchhunt / San Francisco locale**
Goodbye, Lover** (1999) Roland Joffé **Femme fatale / blackmail / murder**
Goodfellas**** (1990) Martin Scorsese **Biopic / ex-mobster Henry Hill**
Good Night, My Love** (1972) Peter Hyams **PI and partner look for missing persons / retro 1940s noir / TV**
A Good Night to Die (2003) Craig Singer **One hit man saves another**
Gotham* (1988) Lloyd Fonvielle **PI tracks down greedy femme fatale**
Grosse Point Blank** (1997) George Armitage **Hit man at high school re-union**
Guilty as Sin** (1993) Sidney Lumet **Lawyer accused of murdering wife**
A Gun, a Car, a Blonde** (1998) Stefani Ames **Paraplegic's noir fantasy**

*Guncrazy*** (1992) Tamra Davis **Abused girl kills rapist / fugitive couple**
Gunn (1967) Blake Edwards **(TV) PI hired to find gangster's killer**
*Hammett*** (1982) Wim Wenders **Crime writer solves complex mystery /
biopic**
*The Hand That Rocks the Cradle*** (1992) Curtis Hanson **Hellish nanny
invades unsuspecting family**
The Hanged Man (1964) Michael Caffey **Born-again hero escapes death**
*Hard Contract** (1969) S. G. Pogostin **Thriller / hit man in love in Europe**
*Hardcore*** (1979) Paul Schrader **Kidnapped teen becomes porn star**
*Hard Eight*** (1997) Paul T. Anderson **Reno gamblers / hookers /
malevolence**
*Hard Target*** (1993) John Woo **Van Damme thriller in bayous / violence**
*Harper*** (1966) Jack Smight **Los Angeles PI investigates disappearances**
*Heat*** (1995) Michael Mann **Thief (De Niro) vs. cop (Pacino) / heist**
*Heat Wave*** (1982) Philip Noyce **Land swindle and murder in Australia**
Heaven (1999) Scott Reynolds **Gambler falls for stripper / flashbacks**
*Heavenly Creatures*** (1994) Peter Jackson **Two teens kill mother in
New Zealand**
*Heaven's Prisoners*** (1996) Phil Joanou **New Orleans PI / drugs / murder**
*Henry, Portrait of a Serial Killer*** (1989) James McNaughton **Biopic /
mindless murder sprees**
Henry, Portrait of a Serial Killer, Part II (1996) Chuck Parello **Arsonist
joins killer**
Hickey and Boggs (1972) Robert Culp **Two PIs track down murderers**
*The Hit*** (1985) Stephen Frears **Hit man and hooker in Spain**
Hit List (1988) William Lustig **Mafia kidnappings / victims recovered**
Hit Me (1996) Stephen Shainberg **Double dealing / double cross thriller**
*Homicide*** (1991) David Mamet **Jewish cop looks into anti-Semitic
crimes**
*The Honeymoon Killers*** (1969) Leonard Kastle **Gigolo and nurse mur-
der for cash**
Hoodlum (1997) Bill Duke **Biopic / 1930s black gangster stops the New
York City mob**
*The Hoodlum Priest*** (1961) Irvin Kershner **Biopic / Father Clark and
teens**
*The Hot Spot*** (1990) Dennis Hopper **Texas drifter / femme fatale /
heist**
House of Cards (1968) Michael Lessac **Amnesia noir / murder in Mexico**
*House of Games*** (1987) David Mamet **Femme psychiatrist researches
crime**

The House on Carroll Street** (1988) Peter Yates **Nazi paranoia / 1950s New York City / FBI / smuggling refugees**

The House on Turk Street (2002) Bob Rafelson **Hammett story / cop captured by thieves during bank heist / seduced by femme pianist**

Hush, Hush, Sweet Charlotte* (1964) Robert Aldrich **Southern gothic / sister discovers murderer**

Hustle** (1975) Robert Aldrich **Los Angeles detective uncovers call girl murder**

I, the Jury** (1982) Richard T. Heffron **Color remake / Mike Hammer discovers murderer of best friend**

Illicit Behavior (1991) Worth Keeter **Femme manipulates heirs for two million dollars**

Impulse (1990) Sondra Locke **Femme cop poses as prostitute / thriller**

The Incident** (1967) Larry Peerce **Two New York City thugs take over subway train**

In Cold Blood*** (1967) Richard Brooks **Docu-noir / two cons kill Kansas family**

Innocents with Dirty Hands (1975) Claude Chabrol **Sex triangle / murder**

The Insider** (2002) Michael Mann **Whistle-blower / tobacco industry**

Internal Affairs*** (1990) Mike Figgis **Los Angeles corrupt cop / thriller**

In the Company of Men**** (1996) Neil LaBute **Corporate chicanery / victims**

In the Heat of the Night** (1967) Norman Jewison **Mississippi murders / Mr. Tibbs investigates**

Intimate Obsession (1992) Lawrence Ungar **Married couple seek love elsewhere, leading to divorce and murder**

Intimate Stranger** (1961) Joseph Losey **Woman claims to be wife of film director**

The Jackal (1997) Michael Caton-Jones **Poor remake of *The Day of the Jackal* / hit man and IRA target / completely fictional neo-noir thriller**

Jackie Brown** (1997) Quentin Tarantino **Black stewardess / gun runners / Mexico locale / from Elmore Leonard novel**

Jade (1995) William Friedkin **San Francisco cop / axe murder / kinky sex / politics**

Jagged Edge** (1985) Richard Marquand **Femme lawyer defends murderer**

Jezebel's Kiss (1990) Harvey Keith **Small-town beauty destroys men**

Johnny Cool (1963) William Asher **Sicilian bandit seeks revenge in United States**

Johnny Handsome** (1989) Walter Hill **Plastic surgery and revenge thriller**

Johnny Mnemonic (1995) Robert Longo **Sci-fi / corporation seeks computer freak**

Johnny Skidmarks (1998) John Raffo **Photographer employed by blackmailers**

Joy Ride** (2001) John Dahl **Three teens victimized by hostile hitchhiker**

Juice (1992) Ernest R. Dickerson **Three Harlem youths earn respect / guns**

Kafka** (1991) Steven Soderbergh **Clerk drawn into anarchist plot / biopic**

Kalifornia** (1993) Dominic Sena **Road movie / two couples / photographers and killers**

The Killer inside Me** (1976) Burt Kennedy **Nevada sheriff becomes psychotic killer**

The Killers** (1964) Don Siegel **Color remake / insurance man seeks arch-heist man while investigating auto mechanic's death**

The Killing of a Chinese Bookie* (1976) John Cassavetes **Loan sharks / Asian mob**

The Killing Time (1987) Rick King **California murders / blackmail / sex**

Killing Zoe** (1994) Roger Avary **Bank heist / drugs / sex / Paris locale**

Kill Me Again** (1990) John Dahl **Detective fakes femme fatale's murder**

The Kill-off** (1989) Maggie Greenwald **Femme gossip causes havoc / New Jersey**

The King of Marvin Gardens** (1972) Bob Rafelson **Bad brother runs black crime syndicate**

King of New York** (1990) Abel Ferrara **Drug czar reigns over New York City mob**

A Kiss before Dying** (1991) James Dearden **Climber kills for wealth**

Kiss Me a Killer (1991) Marcus de Leon **Latino lovers plot husband's death**

Kiss Me, Kill Me*** (1976) Michael O'Herlihy **District attorney tracks killer of Aussie schoolteacher**

Kiss of Death** (1995) Barbet Schroeder **Color remake / car thief informs**

Kiss or Kill** (1997) Bill Bennett **Cops on trail of Aussie murderers**

Kiss the Girls** (1997) Gary Fleder **Cop looks for femme serial killer**

Kitten with a Whip (1964) Douglas Heyes **Femme juvenile delinquent ruins politico's life**

*Klute*** (1971) Alan J. Pakula **Cop searches for stalker of prostitute**

*The Krays*** (1990) Peter Medak **British twins / color gangster noir / 1960s**

*The Kremlin Letter** (1970) John Huston **Cold War / espionage neo-noir**

Lady Beware (1987) Karen Arthur **Psychotic doctor obsessed with erotic gal**

*Lady in Cement** (1968) Gordon Douglas **Miami PI finds corpse / perp**

*The Last Boy Scout*** (1991) Tony Scott **PI and football player team up against legalized sports gambling**

*The Last Embrace*** (1979) Jonathan Demme **PI's wife killed / Niagara Falls locale**

*Last Exit to Brooklyn*** (1989) Uli Edel **Brooklyn prostitute and Mafia**

*Last Man Standing** (1996) Damian Lee **Texas gangster / western / *Yojimbo* inspired**

Last Way Out (1997) Mark Steensland **Retro 1940s black-and-white noir love story**

*The Late Show*** (1977) Robert Benton **Comic noir parody / PI and femme**

*Leaving Las Vegas*** (1995) Mike Figgis **Dark noir / alcoholic suicide**

*Lepke** (1975) Menahem Golan **Biopic / retro 1920s / colorful gangster noir**

*Lethal Weapon*** (1987) Richard Donner **Ex–Vietnam vets / corrupt cops / heroin ring**

Lethal Weapon 2 (1989) Richard Donner **Cops break smuggling ring**

Lethal Weapon 3 (1992) Richard Donner **Cops expose bad cops and arms racket**

Lethal Weapon 4 (1998) Richard Donner **Cops tangle with Asian gang lord**

*Let Him Have It*** (1991) Peter Medak **British law unjustly executes re-tarded man**

*Let No Man Write My Epitaph*** (1960) Philip Leacock **Chicago junkie mom raises teen son / pianist becomes gangster**

Let the Devil Wear Black (1999) Stacy Title ***Hamlet* recycled / noir**

*Liebestraum**** (1991) Mike Figgis **Triangle reduplicates forty-year-old murder**

Light Sleeper (1992) Paul Schrader **Boss puts drug courier out of job**

*The Limey**** (1999) Steven Soderbergh **British ex-con visits Los Angeles / looks into murder of daughter / drugs**

*Little Odessa*** (1995) James Gray **Soviet gangster returns to Brighton**

*Lone Star**** (1996) John Sayles **Texas sheriff tracks down murderer**

*The Longest Night** (1997) Jack Smight **Wealthy kidnapped girl placed in underground coffin**

*The Long Goodbye** (1973) Robert Altman **Parody of PI Philip Marlowe**

*The Long Good Friday*** (1980) John MacKenzie **London crime boss betrayed**

*The Long Kiss Goodnight*** (1996) Renny Harlin **Femme amnesia victim was CIA operative / ultraviolent neo-noir**

*Lost Highway*** (1987) David Lynch **Murderer melds with mechanic / fantasy**

*Love at Large*** (1990) Alan Rudolph **Lovers hire detectives / crisscross**

*Love Crimes** (1992) Lizzie Borden **Photographer rapes women / district attorney investigates**

*Love Walked In*** (1997) Juan J. Campanella **Piano player / femme / detective / get-rich-quick scheme**

Lulu on the Bridge (1998) Paul Auster **Burnt-out saxophonist / dead body**

*Madigan*** (1968) Don Siegel **Cops lose guns to sadistic murderer**

*Magnum Force*** (1973) Ted Post **Dirty Harry tracks down vigilante cops**

Malice (1993) Harold Becker **Evil surgeon intrudes on college professor and wife / startling thriller**

Malone (1987) Harley Cokliss **Ex–CIA man stumbles into swindle / Oregon**

*The Manchurian Candidate**** (2004) Jonathan Demme **Political paranoia remake set after Persian Gulf War / microchips in place of brainwashing**

*Manhunter*** (1986) Michael Mann **Red Dragon serial killer vs. FBI**

Man on Fire (2004) Tony Scott **Alcoholic ex-PI searches for kidnapped youngster in Mexico**

*Man-trap*** (1961) Edmond O'Brien **Ex-soldier lured into hijack / tragic results**

Man with a Gun (1995) David Wyles **Hit man hired to kill gang moll**

*Marathon Man*** (1976) John Schlesinger **Nazi criminal exposed by runner**

*Marlowe** (1969) Paul Bogart **Chandler's PI hired to find missing heir**

*Married to the Mob*** (1988) Jonathan Demme **Mafia comedy neo-noir**

*Masquerade*** (1988) Bob Swaim **Gigolo plots murder of wealthy wife**

*The Matrix*** (1999) Andy and Larry Wachowski **Sci-fi noir / a hacker is destined to save the world**

*McCabe and Mrs. Miller*** (1972) Robert Altman **Gunfighter sets up brothels**

The Mean Season** (1985) Philip Borsos **Miami news hack speaks for psycho / murderer**

Mean Streets** (1973) Martin Scorsese **Wise-guy antics in Little Italy**

Menace II Society (1993) Allen Hughes **Black Los Angeles teens / thefts / murder**

Miami Blues** (1990) George Armitage **Killer on run uses prostitute**

Miami Vice: The Movie* (1984) Thomas Carter **Cop buddies solve crimes**

Mickey One** (1965) Arthur Penn **Actor runs to escape mob in Chicago**

Midnight in the Garden of Good and Evil*** (1997) Clint Eastwood **Gay man kills lover in Savannah / courtroom neo-noir**

Midnight Lace* (1960) David Miller **Woman menaced by unknown stalker**

Mike's Murder* (1984) James Bridges **Woman investigates lover's death**

Mikey and Nicky* (1976) Elaine May **Two men spend one night dodging hit man**

Miller's Crossing*** (1990) Joel Coen **Politician caught in crossfire of gangsters / remake of Hammett's *The Glass Key***

Mirage** (1965) Edward Dmytryk **Amnesiac becomes target of New York City manhunt**

Mirage** (1995) Edward James Olmos ***Vertigo* remake / cop falls for fatal dame**

The Mommy (1995) Max Allan Collins **Schoolteacher stalked by crazy mom**

The Money Trap** (1966) Burt Kennedy **Cop's greed leads to death / crime**

The Morning After** (1986) Sidney Lumet **Alcoholic dame finds corpse**

Mortal Passions** (1990) Andrew Lane **Wife manipulates lover / kill spouse**

Mortal Thoughts* (1991) Howard Cummings **New Jersey wives / one husband dead / whodunit**

Mr. Majestyk (1974) Richard Fleischer **Colorado melon grower vs. Mafia**

Mrs. Winterbourne (1996) Richard Benjamin **Comic remake of *No Man of Her Own* / mistaken identity neo-noir**

Ms. 45** (1981) Abel Ferrera **Mute woman raped twice / revenge**

Mugshot (1996) Matt Mahurin **Amnesiac's relationship with black man**

Mulholland Drive*** (2001) David Lynch **Amnesiac actress recovers career**

Mulholland Falls*** (1996) Lee Tamahori **Retro 1940s noir / gangsters killed**

Murder, Inc.** (1960) Burt Balaban **Gangster Abe Rellis is murdered in Coney Island's Half-Moon Hotel**

Murder in the First** (1994) Marc Rocco **Prison noir / warden's injustices**

Murphy's Law* (1986) J. Lee Thompson **Los Angeles cop victim of a frame-up**

The Music of Chance** (1993) Philip Haas **Unlucky gamblers forced to build wall**

Mute Witness* (1995) Anthony Waller **Makeup artist sees slasher murder**

Nails (1992) Dennis Hopper **Cop's revenge for partner killed by dealer**

Narrow Margin** (1990) Peter Hyams **Color remake / cop protects witness**

Natural Born Killers*** (1994) Oliver Stone **Serial killer couple and media**

New Jack City (1991) Mario Van Peebles **Harlem drug lord vs. cops**

New York, New York** (1977) Martin Scorsese **Gotham romance / musical noir / fatal ending**

Nick of Time (1995) John Badham **Murder of California governor tied to kidnapping**

Night and the City (1992) Irwin Winkler **Bad remake / hustler loses to mob**

Night Falls on Manhattan** (1997) Sidney Lumet **District attorney covers for corrupt cop**

Night of the Following Day (1968) Hubert Cornfield **Americans kidnap French girl at Orly Airport / ransom / murder**

Night of the Hunter (1991) David Greene **Poor TV remake / preacher terrorizes children for hidden fortune**

Nightwatch* (1998) Ole Bornedal **Morgue guard terrorized by psychotic**

No Mercy* (1986) Richard Pearce **Chicago cop in Cajun bayou / revenge**

Normal Life (1996) John McNaughton **Biopic / woman brings honest cop down / real-life story of Illinois killers Jeffrey and Jill Erickson**

Notorious (1992) Colin Bucksey **Poor TV color remake / Paris / gunrunning**

No Way Out*** (1987) Roger Donaldson **Remake of *The Big Clock* / undercover mole sought by FBI / murder and politics in Washington**

Object of Obsession (1995) Alex Gregory **Divorcée / psycho / revenge**

Obsession** (1976) Brian De Palma **Southerner meets kidnapped wife abroad**

Once a Thief** (1965) Ralph Nelson **Ex-con hounded by vengeful cop**

Once upon a Time in America** (1984) Sergio Leone **Gangster epic**

One False Move*** (1991) Carl Franklin **Road movie / two killers on the run / black femme fatale**

One Tough Cop* (1998) Bruno Barreto **Biopic / cop uncovers Harlem rapes**

The Onion Field (1979) Harold Becker **True crime / two cops murdered**

Ordeal (1973) Lee H. Katzin **Husband left in desert by wife and lover**

The Outfit** (1974) John Flynn **Robber paroled / avenges brother's death**

Out of Bounds* (1986) Richard Tuggle **Los Angeles family picks wrong bag / drugs / crimes / murder**

Out of Sight** (1998) Steven Soderbergh **Femme cop brings in bank robber**

Out of the Dark (1989) Michael Schroeder **Telephone sex / clown-masked killer / carnage galore**

Out of the Rain (1990) Gary Winick **Couple trapped / drugs in small town**

Pacific Heights** (1990) John Schlesinger **Tenant from hell in San Francisco**

Palmetto** (1998) Volker Schlondorff **Ex-con / femme fatale / kidnap scheme**

Palookaville (1995) Alan Taylor **Unemployed trio uses crime for cash**

Panic in the Year Zero (1962) Ray Milland **Sci-fi noir / nuked family / survival**

The Parallax View*** (1974) Alan J. Pakula **Political killings in Seattle**

Past Midnight (1992) Jan Eliasberg **Social worker and psycho ex-convict in love**

Patriot Games** (1992) Philip Noyce **Thriller / CIA agent saves English queen from IRA assassination**

Payback** (1999) Brian Helgeland **Color remake of *Point Blank* / felon wants cash from mob**

Pay or Die** (1960) Richard Wilson **New York City detective pursues Black Hand**

The Pelican Brief** (1993) Alan J. Pakula **Hit men stalk law student / conspiracy thriller**

Performance* (1970) Nicholas Roeg **Gangster lives with pop star / drugs**

Phoenix* (1998) Danny Cannon **Arizona gambling cop in debt to loan sharks**

Phone Booth** (2003) Joel Schumacher **Publicist humiliated by stalker**

P.I.** (1987) Nigel Dick **Corrupt drug-dealing cops stalked by FBI**

The Player** (1992) Robert Altman **Hollywood executive eludes prosecution**

Playing God (1996) Andy Wilson **Druggie surgeon works for gangster**

Point Break (1991) Kathryn Bigelow **FBI infiltrates surfer gang**

Point of No Return (1993) John Badham **Femme felon becomes assassin / American remake of French film *La Femme Nikita***

Poodle Springs** (1998) Bob Rafelson **Chandler's unfinished novel completed for TV / Philip Marlowe is married with mistress**

Portrait in Black** (1960) Michael Gordon **Wife convinces doctor to kill spouse / the old, old story**

Positive I.D. (1987) Andy Anderson **Raped woman seeks revenge**

The Postman Always Rings Twice*** (1981) Bob Rafelson **Color remake / drifter kills husband for money and sex / 1930s noir ambience recaptured**

Presumed Innocent*** (1990) Alan J. Pakula **Dallying district attorney accused of murder**

Pretty Boy Floyd (1961) Herbert J. Leder **Biopic / violent black-and-white noir**

Pretty Poison** (1968) Noel Black **Arsonist teams with teenager / murder**

Primal Fear* (1996) Gregory Hoblit **Chicago district attorney defends clergy murderer**

Prince of the City** (1981) Sidney Lumet **Cop becomes drug informant**

Prizzi's Honor*** (1985) John Huston **Parody / gangster noir**

The Professional** (1994) Luc Besson **French hit man teams with teenager**

Psycho* (1998) Gus Van Sant **Dreadful color remake about serial killer**

Psycho II (1983) Richard Franklin **Norman Bates goes home after twenty-two years**

Psycho III (1986) Anthony Perkins **Bates is drawn to mother figure**

Psycho IV (1990) Mick Garris **Norman recounts his childhood / prequel**

Psychopath (1997) Max Fischer **Professor enlists help of serial killer to solve law school murders**

The Public Eye** (1992) Howard Franklin **Homage to Weegee / news crime photographer supreme**

Pulp Fiction*** (1994) Quentin Tarantino **Three crime stories intertwined / shifts in time and narration / violence combined with 1970s pop**

Pusher (1996) Nicholas W. Refn **Dealer in Copenhagen / violence / drugs**

Q & A** (1990) Sidney Lumet **Corrupt cop murders dealer / claims self-defense**

A Rage in Harlem* (1991) Bill Duke **Femme crook dupes black gangsters**

Raging Bull*** (1980) Martin Scorsese **Biopic / Jake LaMotta / boxing noir**

The Rain Killer (1990) Ken Stein **Cops track serial killer**

Ransom** (1996) Ron Howard **Superior remake / millionaire refuses payment**

Ratchet** (1998) John Johnson **Blocked screenwriter rents house in Nantucket / serial killers show up**

*The Real McCoy** (1993) Russell Mulcahy **Femme bank robber wants to go straight / son kidnapped / another heist**

*Rear Window** (1998) Ken Kelsch **TV remake / wheelchair-bound voyeur / murder**

*Red Rock West*** (1993) John Dahl **Oil rigger mistaken for hit man / Wyoming**

*Reflections of Murder** (1974) John Badham **Two femme teachers kill headmaster / jealousy / lesbianism / color remake of French original *Diabolique***

*Reindeer Games** (2000) John Frankenheimer **Convicts rob Indian casino**

*Relentless** (1989) William Lustig **Rejected Los Angeles cop turns serial killer**

Rent-a-Cop (1988) Jerry London **Security cop tracks down drugs, killers**

*Revenge*** (1990) Tony Scott **Thief falls for femme / almost kills husband**

*The Rich Man's Wife*** (1996) Amy Holden **Bored wife and barfly plan murder**

*The Rise and Fall of Legs Diamond*** (1960) Bud Boetticher **Gangster biopic**

*Rising Sun*** (1993) Philip Kaufman **Prostitute killed / U.S. cops in Japan**

*River of Grass*** (1995) Kelly Reichardt **Florida noir / lovers kill mistakenly**

*The River Wild*** (1994) Curtis Hanson **Criminals take over family whitewater expedition**

*Robocop*** (1987) Paul Verhoeven **Detroit cop rewired / fights crime / sci-fi**

Robocop 2 (1990) Irvin Kershner **Robocop battles criminal cyborg**

Robocop 3 (1993) Fred Dekker **Japs pit Robocop against android ninja**

*Rolling Thunder*** (1977) John Flynn **War vet is vigilante / family killed**

*Romeo Is Bleeding*** (1993) Peter Medak **Corrupt cop hired to kill femme**

*The Rosary Murders*** (1987) Fred Walton **Priest private eye looks into church murders**

Rough Magic (1997) Clare Peploe **Rich man hires reporter to track fiancée in Mexico who possesses magical powers**

Ruby (1992) John MacKenzie **Fictional noir about Kennedy assassination**

Run (1991) Geoff Burrowes **Law student causes death of gangster's son**

*Rush** (1991) Paul Sylbert **Two undercover narcs become addicts / depressing**

The Salton Sea* (2002) D. J. Caruso **Recovering California addicts / sleazy noir**

Scarface** (1983) Brian De Palma **Retro 1920s noir / Cuban gangster epic / incest / drugs**

Scissors (1991) Frank D. Felitta **Woman driven mad by trauma / lovers**

Scotch and Milk** (1998) Adam Goldberg **Man looks for love / finds murder**

Séance on a Wet Afternoon*** (1964) Bryan Forbes **Psychic searches for fame through bogus kidnapping / British neo-noir**

Sea of Love** (1989) Harold Becker **Cop falls for lonely hearts serial killer**

Second Skin (2000) Darrell Roodt **Femme amnesia victim helped by lover, a bookstore owner drawn back into a life of crime**

Secret Games (1992) Alex Hippolyte **Woman moonlights as prostitute / marriage and identity are threatened**

Serial Mom** (1994) John Waters **Femme kills when life is "interrupted"**

Serpico*** (1973) Sidney Lumet **Biopic / undercover cop exposes corruption**

Se7en**** (1995) David Fincher **Serial killer caught by crime pattern / dark**

Sexual Malice* (1994) Jag Mundhra **Bored wife / affair / murder**

Shaft** (1971) Gordon Parks **First black PI film / child kidnapped**

Shaft* (2000) John Singleton **Reprise / Black PI tracks child murderer**

Shaft in Africa* (1973) John Guillermin **PI helps stop slave trading**

Shaft's Big Score* (1972) Gordon Parks **PI prevents murder in Brooklyn**

Shallow Grave*** (1994) Danny Boyle **Three roommates find drug money**

Sharkey's Machine** (1981) Burt Reynolds **Undercover cop hunts crime czar**

Shattered** (1991) Wolfgang Peterson **Recovering accident victim / unfaithful wife / stolen identity**

Shock Corridor** (1963) Sam Fuller **Sane reporter turns mad in asylum**

Shoot to Kill* (1988) Roger Spottiswoode **Two cops hunt killer in mountains of Pacific Northwest**

The Silence of the Lambs**** (1991) Jonathan Demme **Femme FBI agent tracks serial killer with aid of demented psychiatrist**

The Silent Partner (1978) Daryl Duke **Teller foils theft / takes money**

A Simple Plan** (1998) Sam Raimi **Four million dollars found in Minnesota plane crash / greed**

The Singing Detective** (1986) Jon Amiel **British TV detective dreams he's Philip Marlowe / five hours of imaginary exploits confined in hospital**

The Singing Detective* (2003) Keith Gordon **Two-hour version of British classic / patient hallucinates musical numbers and femmes fatales**

Single White Female** (1992) Barbet Schroeder **Roommate from hell**

Sisters* (1973) Brian De Palma **Good and evil sister-twins cause havoc**

Sky Captain and the World of Tomorrow (2004) Kenny Conran **Pulp neo-noir / highly stylized comic book dialogue and action in black and white and color**

Slamdance (1987) Wayne Wang **Cartoonist blamed for murder / killer lurks**

Sleepers* (1996) Barry Levinson **Four teens abused / take revenge on cops**

Sleeping with the Enemy** (1991) Joseph Ruben **Woman escapes psycho mate**

Sliver (1993) Philip Noyce **Sex, voyeurism, and murder in posh Manhattan**

Someone to Watch Over Me* (1987) Ridley Scott **Married cop falls for woman in witness protection**

Something Wild** (1986) Jonathan Demme **Ménage à trois road movie comedy leads to incredible violence**

Sorcerer** (1977) William Friedkin **Four men drive nitro-loaded trucks in South America / tragic dark consequences / remake of *Wages of Fear***

Soylent Green (1972) Richard Fleischer **Sci-fi / murders lead detectives to discovery of green food for twenty-first century**

The Spanish Prisoner** (1998) David Mamet **Industrial espionage con**

Special Delivery (1976) Paul Wendkos **Three unemployed vets rob bank**

The Split (1968) Gordon Flemyng **Black con robs Los Angeles Coliseum during football game**

Stakeout (1987) John Badham **Two cops / femme fatale / looking for quarry**

State of Grace** (1990) Phil Joanou **Cop returns to inform on Irish mob**

The State of Things* (1982) Wim Wenders **Los Angeles director tracks down producer who abandoned film crew in Portugal**

The Stepfather* (1987) Joseph Ruben **Homicidal nut / "perfect" family**

Still of the Night* (1982) Robert Benton **Psychiatrist loves killer?**

The Stone Killer (1973) Michael Winner **Cops vs. Mafia / mass killings**

Stormy Monday** (1988) Mike Figgis **U.S. developer vs. Newcastle gambler**

Storyville (1992) Mark Frost **Political blackmail / murder in New Orleans**

Straight Time* (1978) Ulu Grosbard **Ex-con reverts to life of crime**

Strange Days* (1995) Kathryn Bigelow **Los Angeles cop peddles snuff tapes**

Stranger's Kiss (1984) Matthew Chapman **Director encourages actors' offscreen romance / disastrous results**

Street of No Return** (1989) Sam Fuller **Pop singer's throat cut by gangster / revenge**

Striking Distance (1993) Rowdy Herrington **Pittsburgh cop vs. serial killer**

Stripped to Kill (1987) Katt Shea **Femme cop goes after psycho killer**

St. Valentine's Day Massacre* (Roger Corman) **Retro 1920s / revisionist**

Sudden Impact** (1983) Clint Eastwood **Dirty Harry vs. revenge-obsessed murderess**

Sugar Hill** (1993) Leon Ichaso **Two brothers / Harlem drug empire / one leaves**

Sunset Grill (1992) Kevin Connor **Cop looks for wife's killer / meets femme fatale / Mexican locale**

Suspect (1987) Peter Yates **District attorney and lobbyist look for murderer in DC**

Suture (1993) Scott McGehee **Mistaken identity swap / murder / amnesia**

Swimming with Sharks*** (1995) George Huang **Hollywood gofer gets revenge**

Swoon** (1992) Tom Kalin **Neo-noir rendering of 1924 Leopold Loeb case**

The Talented Mr. Ripley** (1999) Anthony Minghella **Best friend kills heir for sybaritic lifestyle and femme / remake of French *Plein Soleil***

Tango and Cash* (1989) Andre Konchalovsky **Los Angeles cops go after drug lord**

The Temp* (1993) Tom Holland **Femme slithers up corporate ladder / murder**

10 to Midnight** (1983) J. Lee Thompson **Cop goes after stalker / serial killer**

Tequila Sunrise** (1988) Robert Towne **Drug dealer and cop / friends in love with same woman**

The Terminator*** (1984) James Cameron **Sci-fi noir / cyborg killer sent to destroy future liberator**

Terminator II: Judgment Day* (1991) James Cameron **Sequel / cyborg confronts another killing machine to protect liberator**

Terminator III: Rise of the Machines* (2003) Jonathan Mostow **A femme Terminator is after the liberator / cyborg defends him and the world**

Thelma and Louise**** (1991) Ridley Scott **Two southern gals bond / a femme road movie / commit petty crimes / leads to tragic consequences**

Thief** (1981) Michael Mann **Car thief's last big score before retiring**

Thief of Hearts* (1984) Douglas Day Stewart **Thief steals femme's diary / falls in love / bitter repercussions**

Thieves Like Us** (1974) Robert Altman **Fugitive couple rob banks / 1930s**

The Thin Blue Line** (1988) Errol Morris **Documentary recreation / wrong man theme**

Things to Do in Denver When You're Dead** (1995) Gary Fleder **Neo-noir / gangster tries to go straight / surreal results**

Third Degree Burn (1989) Roger Spottiswoode **PI follows woman / femme's husband is killed**

The Third Voice* (1960) Hubert Cornfield **Woman kills lover / boyfriend impersonates him for the money**

This World, Then the Fireworks* (1997) Michael Oblowitz **Pulp drama / incest / robbery / murder**

The Thomas Crown Affair** (1968) Norman Jewison **Perfect bank heist almost foiled by femme detective**

The Thomas Crown Affair** (1999) John McTiernan **Recycled neo-noir / playboy steals art treasure / femme detectives seeks paintings**

Thunderheart (1992) Michael Apted **PI looks for murder in Sioux Reservation**

Tightrope* (1984) Richard Tuggle **Cop pursues killer of prostitutes / New Orleans**

To Die For** (1995) Gus Van Sant **Seduction / murder in media / black comedy**

Tom Horn** (1980) William Wiard **Noir gunman stops rustlers / Wyoming**

Tough Guys Don't Dance* (1987) Norman Mailer **Amnesiac commits murder?**

Track 29* (1988) Nicholas Roeg **Femme seduces stranger / husband plays with toy trains**

Training Day** (2001) Antoine Fuqua **Bad cop tries to corrupt partner**

Trainspotting** (1995) Danny Boyle **Amoral, nihilistic Scottish youth on run / drugs**

Trespass (1992) Walter Hill **Firemen search for gold / gangster rivals**

Trial by Jury* (1994) Heywood Gould **Mother and son threatened by gangster**

The Trigger Effect* (1996) David Koepp **Blackout causes tension / murder in Southern California**

Trouble in Mind* (1986) Alan Rudolph **Ex-cop is involved with crook**

True Believer** (1989) Joseph Ruben **1960s radical lawyer takes on Asian mob / pseudo–William Kunstler biopic**

True Confessions** (1981) Ulu Grosbard **Priest and cop (brothers) pitted against each other to solve a crime**

True Crime** (1999) Clint Eastwood **Boozy ex-reporter saves innocent man**

True Romance** (1993) Tony Scott **Teens steal cocaine and head for Los Angeles**

12 Monkeys (1995) Terry Gilliam **Sci-fi noir / virologists investigate dementia**

28 Days Later** (2003) Danny Boyle **Horror noir / men into savages from bites**

Twilight* (1998) Robert Benton **Retired cops / PIs handle blackmail payoff**

Twin Falls, Idaho (1999) Michael Polish **Hooker falls for one twin / noirish situation**

Twisted (2004) Philip Kaufman **Woman in distress vs. serial killer**

Two Days in the Valley* (1996) John Herzfeld **Hit man in San Fernando**

The Two Jakes** (1990) Jack Nicholson **Jake Gittes returns to Chinatown to solve murder ten years later**

Ulee's Gold*** (1997) Victor Nunez **Beekeeper saves son from thugs**

Undercurrent (1998) Frank Kerr **Undercover cop blackmailed into affair with gangster's wife**

The Underneath** (1995) Steven Soderbergh **Gambler enters into armored car robbery for love / color remake of *Criss Cross***

Under Suspicion* (1992) Simon Moore **Divorce-scam artists find murder**

Underworld (1996) Roger Christian **Ex-con revenges father's death using psychology**

Unforgettable* (1996) John Dahl **Husband uses memory transference to find wife's killer**

Union City* (1980) Mark Reichert **Film noir spoof of fugitive couple**

Unlawful Entry** (1992) Jonathan Kaplan **Cop seduces wife of complainant / revenge**

The Untouchables* (1987) Brian De Palma **Nostalgic G-man / gangster noir**

U-Turn** (1997) Oliver Stone **Gambler stranded in Arizona meets couple who need a hit man**

Vigilante (1983) William Lustig **Ex-cop joins vigilante squad**

V.I. Warshawski (1991) Jeff Kanew **Female PI investigates murders**

Vortex (1983) Scott B. and Beth B. **Punk femme PI investigates murders**

Warning Shot (1967) Buzz Kulik **Trigger-happy Los Angeles cop**

Way of the Gun* (2000) Christopher McQuarrie **Kidnap of surrogate mother by abulic criminals**

What Ever Happened to Baby Jane?* (1962) Robert Aldrich **Southern gothic / murder leads to insanity**

When Strangers Appear (2001) Scott Reynolds **Man is chased by murderers into Aussie roadside diner**

Where the Money Is* (2000) Marek Kaniveska **Bank robber fakes stroke for one last heist**

While You Were Sleeping* (1995) John Turteltaub **Mugging leads to mistaken identity / comedy noir**

Whispers in the Dark (1992) Christopher Crowe **Psychiatrist counsels patient whose lover is ex-murderer**

White of the Eye (1987) Donald Cammell **Innocent man's search for serial killer to prove innocence**

White Sands** (1992) Roger Donaldson **Cop finds dead man, half-million dollars on Indian reservation / whodunit**

Who Framed Roger Rabbit?*** (1988) Robert Zemeckis **Cartoon / live action / 1940s styled retro noir**

Who Killed Teddy Bear?* (1965) Joseph Cates **Busboy and cop are obsessed by pornography, sex, voyeurism / New York City Broadway locale**

Who'll Stop the Rain** (1978) Karel Reisz **Vietnam vet smuggles heroin / violence**

Wild at Heart** (1991) David Lynch **Fugitive couple involve others in their affairs / cross-country trek**

Wild Things** (1998) John McNaughton **Miami cop / abduction / sex / murder**

Witch Hunt (1994) Paul Schrader **Retro 1950s PI solves murder case**

With a Friend Like Harry** (2001) Dominik Moll **Murderous school chum takes over family**

Witness** (1985) Peter Weir **Pennsylvania cop protects Amish child witness to murder**

Wonderland** (2003) James Cox **Biopic / ex–porn star John Holmes / murder**

Wrong Man (1994) Jim McBride **Sailor framed for murder hitches ride with fugitive couple**

Wrong Number (2001) Richard Middleton **Greed results in murder with Internet stock transactions**

X-Files: Fight the Future** (1998) Rob Bowman **FBI agents battle global conspiracy / abductions into space**

The Yakuza** (1975) Sydney Pollack **U.S. vet rescues kidnapped child from Japanese mob**

The Yards*** (2000) James Gray **Ex-con in Queens tries to go straight in spite of criminal family**

Year of the Dragon (1985) Michael Cimino **New York Police Department vs. gangs in Chinatown**

The Young Savages** (1961) John Frankenheimer **Juvenile crime in East Harlem / courtroom drama**

Zero Effect* (1998) Jake Kasdan **PI investigates blackmail in Oregon timber country**

~

Appendix A: Conference Notes
and Other Sources

For the record, I thought I would include my notes in this volume regarding a conference I attended on April 30, 1997, at the French Institute in New York City entitled "Neo-Noir." Some of the opinions of the scholars attending have changed over the past several years—but it is interesting to see their reactions to the meanings of "noir" and "neo-noir."

I. Conference Notes

Neo-noir . . . neo-noir . . . what does this term mean, "neo-noir"? At the French Institute in Manhattan, I was fortunate to attend a panel discussion entitled "Neo-noir" on one very overcast afternoon. One of the panel participants was Paul Schrader, the at-one-time lionized professor of film, film noir critic, and more recently writer and director of a group of films, notably *Taxi Driver* (1974). He said, "Film noir was an American stylistic movement restricted by time and place (1941–1958). Its signposts were *The Maltese Falcon* and *Touch of Evil*—black-and-white films only (no color films noirs), no non-American or foreign films noirs—and pulling a style like this into the present is not good . . . we do *not* have neo-noir, only ironic cinema." Schrader cited *Pulp Fiction* (1994) as his chief example.

Michael Chapman, the cinematographer of *Taxi Driver*, added: "Noir is cinematography. The new noir? The soul of film noir is not there . . . film noir was a reaction to a historical situation which does not exist anymore." Agreeing with Paul Schrader, he acknowledged the modern use of cinema techniques, color, and so on. He claimed that the soul of film noir is missing in today's neo-noirs, which he also called "faux noirs."

When Donald Westlake was asked about working on the screenplay of *The Grifters* (1991) and the "noir tradition," he explained that the original writer, Jim Thompson, was himself a noir character, spending a "wrong life, grim, his work undervalued, having too little time for writing, his entire career ignored." Thompson tried to explain the inside to the outsiders— teaching the middle class what's going on at night in American big cities. Unlike mystery writer Eric Ambler (*The Mask of Dimitrios*), who was always aware of the world around him (politics, history, geography), Thompson was aware of the realities of his particular character creations, their particular milieu, but nothing more.

Elise MacAdam, a new filmmaker, said: "There is a lack of sincerity in neo-noirs—pastiche over content. Perhaps we need the creation of new crimes to disturb audiences on the level of the old film noir days—make upsetting films which may restore a kind of romanticism we saw in the glory days of noir."

Michael Chapman decries and denies the existence of neo-noir or faux noir, claiming there is a:

> spiritual bankruptcy in 1990s cinema. The style of neo-noir comes from MTV photographers, presenting a visual mannerism of the age. The new generation of filmmakers are *not* coming from the print media, but from television, which automatically changes the venue of screenwriting or photography. In neo-noir, we are left with an insincere, hollow cinema . . . we need to invent new styles, new genres.

Donald Westlake compared the 1946 and 1981 versions of *The Postman Always Rings Twice*, noting the strength of the "lid of censorship," which brought tension and style to the 1940s version; without "the lid, the 1980s version remains an exercise in voyeurism."

And so in the 1990s films, the roles of men and women are seen through a different sensibility. The panel used *Pulp Fiction* as a leading example. Its members characterized this film as being based on a series of "twisted reflections where mannerism becomes content [leading to rot]; and although the film is very cynical, it does have three happy endings that take place in different parts throughout the deconstructed narrative."

So, in conclusion, the panel felt the core of film noir—viewing the sexual from the male point of view, and the paranoia of the existential hero— *cannot* be replicated in neo-noir. In the neo-noir style of film, there is gender repression and manipulation—with a "killer woman" trying to reclaim the old film noir style in an ironic neo-noir world (as in *Bound* [1990]). But the old film noir, which was intensely misogynist on a primal level, cannot be reclaimed in the new noir of the present. The old B film is decidedly gone, but it finds its venue in cable TV and movies made for television, which try to resurrect (however unsuccessfully) the old styles.

Regarding his stance on neo-noir, Paul Schrader mockingly said of himself, "Perhaps I am a dinosaur." With his position on categorizing as films noirs only those made in black and white, he was callously intransigent. When I suggested that John Stahl's 1946 Fox film, *Leave Her to Heaven*—photographed in gorgeous Technicolor by Leon Shamroy—should be placed in the film noir canon, Schrader, with his purist point of view, was dissuaded from admitting it to the noir pantheon based on purely academic reasons.

Despite the negatives in this summary of the panel discussion, I thought it was relevant to include in some detail, since so few such discussions have taken place. I also wanted to present an outline of some of the events that have precipitated the realization of the critical posture in cinema known as "neo-noir." While all these lionized filmmakers and writers talked about the glory days of film noir, they constantly used the term "neo-noir" or substituted "faux noir" to describe the new style in film that has persisted since film noir's supposed demise in 1958. This critic maintains that the new noir is here to stay, not just as a critical style or (heaven forbid) genre marker, but as a natural cinematic development in its own right. Vive les films neo-noirs!

II. Other Sources Regarding Neo-Noir

A few months previous to the above discussion, in January of 1997, the Film Forum theater in Manhattan began a five-week retrospective of films based on the works of Cain, Chandler, Hammett, and Woolrich, leading off the series with a prerelease cut of Howard Hawks's 1945 version of Chandler's *The Big Sleep*, with eighteen minutes of never-before-seen footage. An accompanying thirty-minute documentary explained the differences between this version and the 1946 print, seen as the definitive one throughout the world. The program notes refer to the series as showcasing "film noir . . . one of America's most distinctive and durable genres." David Kehr in the *Daily News* of January 10, 1997, began his review of the series with these words:

> They've come to be known as "neo-noirs"—the recent movies inspired by Quentin Tarantino's *Reservoir Dogs* and *Pulp Fiction* that have tried to capture

the shadowy look and despairing tone of the classic Hollywood "film noirs" of the late forties and early fifties. But noir is more than a matter of pulling a fedora over your eyes or puffing meaningfully on a Chesterfield. The neo-noirs seldom get beyond the look and the accessories—they're more fashion shoots than films—to find the philosophy behind the attitudes.

This author disagrees entirely with Kehr's view of neo-noirs. But to understand the style and significance of neo-noir, it is always good to refer to the pulp fictions and films of the 1920s through the 1940s.

In an incisive essay entitled "Three Kinds of Noir," in his 1997 edition of his *Video Companion*, film critic Roger Ebert makes the following distinctions: "Neo-noir: films that come out of the way we live now; Dead-pan noir: movies by directors who *could* make a *classic noir*, but they're too hip to play it straight; and finally, classic noir: they begin with costume and set design, use smoky jazz scores, and the characters are led to their destinies by their own weaknesses."

I believe Ebert's words give us the key to neo-noir—"films that come out of the way we live now" but are very much like their stylistic predecessors, films noirs, in showing the dark side of contemporary American life and dreams. Crime, suspense, and thriller movies have been encoded and reinvented by contemporary writers, photographers, directors, actors, and musicians, who use the latest technologies to express the darkest moods and motives of the American character from the 1960s through the present. Neo-noir protagonists reflect the existential bitterness of the earlier noir era and still find themselves doomed to be outside of the social mainstream. In the aggregate they represent a true reflection of the mental aberrations and dysfunctions of an America that is still a nation in uncertain transition. And neo-noir expresses this resurrection of the noir sensibility of the 1940s and 1950s—it revives stylistically and thematically the dark side of the American persona and dream.

One last note: 1997 was a key year for the development of neo-noir as a critical concept. That August, David Schwartz, film curator of the American Museum of the Moving Image, curated a retrospective of thirty-two mainstream theatrical (and television) films in a show called "Nouveau Noir." This show heralded the "re-invigoration of film noir" by contemporary directors inspired by the distinctive noir blend of "romantic fatalism, psychological ambiguity, urban grit and visual inventiveness." Contemporary directors have also made sci-fi noirs, comedy noirs, cartoon noirs, racially motivated noirs, gender-bender noirs, serial-killer noirs, and others in their quest to explore contemporary unrest.

It is unfortunate that David Schwartz began his series with John Boorman's *Point Blank* (1967) and not with the cinematic event that still permeates, resonates in, and really defines the style of neo-noir as we know it today—the release of Alfred Hitchcock's *Psycho* (1960). I consider *Psycho* to be the most beautifully crafted neo-noir of its day, the best ultraviolent film of the century, and the initiator of the serial-killer theme in American cinema. Many other critics prefer to think of *Harper* (1966), starring Paul Newman, as the kickoff film of the new noir cycle, as some believe *The Maltese Falcon* (1941), starring Humphrey Bogart, initiated the beginning of the film noir style. I am certain I will gain detractors by stating that Orson Welles's *Citizen Kane* (1940) and Boris Ingster's *Stranger on the Third Floor* (1940) are the real initiators of the style—as I firmly believe *Psycho* started the neo-noir style as we know it today.

~

Appendix B:
Video and DVD Sources

The following is a list of video and DVD distributors that have large collections of films and titles available by mail or on the Internet:

Alpha Video
www.oldies.com

Amazon
www.amazon.com

Barnes and Noble
www.bn.com

Darker Images Video
P.O. Box 479
Medway, ME 04460
(207) 723-4429
www.darkerimagesvideo.com

DVD Savant
www.dvdsavant.com

Evergreen Video
37 Carmine St.
New York, NY
(212) 691-7632
www.evergreenvideo.com

Facet's Video
1517 W. Fullerton Ave.
Chicago, IL
(800) 331-6197
www.facets.org

Kim's Video
Four stores in New York, NY
www.kimsvideo.com

Kino Video
333 West 39th Street
New York, NY
(800) 562-3330
www.kinovideo.com

TLA Video
521 4th St.
Philadelphia, PA
(800) 333-8521
www.tlavideo.com

~

Select Bibliography

Borde, Raymond, and Etienne Chaumenton. *Panorama du film noir américain*. Paris: Editions du Minuit, 1955.
———. *A Panorama of American Film Noir*. San Francisco: City Lights, 2002.
Cameron, Ian, ed. *The Book of Film Noir*. New York: Continuum, 1992.
Chibnall, Steve, and Robert Murphy, eds. *British Crime Cinema*. London: Routledge, 1999.
Christopher, Nicholas. *Somewhere in the Night: Film Noir and the American City*. New York: Free Press, 1997.
Dickos, Andrew. *Street with No Name: A History of the Classic American Film Noir*. Lexington, KY: University of Kentucky Press, 2002.
Duncan, Paul. *Film Noir: Films of Trust and Betrayal*. London: Pocket Essentials, 2000.
Ebert, Roger. *Roger Ebert's Movie Home Companion*. Kansas City: Andrews and McMeel, 1997.
Erickson, Todd, "Evidence of the Film Noir in Contemporary American Cinema," MA thesis, Brigham Young University, 1988.
Glassman, Steve, and Maurice O'Sullivan, eds. *Florida Noir: Crime Fiction and Film in the Sunshine State*. Bowling Green, OH: Bowling Green State University Press, 1997.
Gorman, Ed, Lee Server, and Martin H. Greenberg, eds. *Big Book of Noir*. New York: Carroll and Graf, 1998.
Greco, J. "File on Robert Siodmak in Hollywood: 1941–1951." At dissertation.com, 1999.
Halliwell, Leslie. *Halliwell's 2002 Film and Video Guide*, 17th ed. Ed. John B. Walker. London: HarperCollins, 2001.

145

Hansberry, Katherine Burroughs. *Bad Boys of Film Noir*. Jefferson, NC: McFarland, 2003.

———. *Femme Noir: Bad Girls of Film Noir*. Jefferson, NC: McFarland, 1998.

Hare, William. *Early Film Noir*. Jefferson, NC: McFarland, 2003.

Haut, Woody. *Hardboiled Fiction: Pop Culture and the Cold War*. London: Serpent's Tail, 1995.

———. *Neo-Noir: Contemporary American Crime Fiction*. London: Serpent's Tail, 1999.

Hirsch, Foster. *Detours and Lost Highways: A Map of Neo-Noir*. New York: Limelight, 1999.

Horsley, Lee. *The Noir Thriller*. London: Palgrave / MacMillan, 2001.

Keany, Michael F. *Film Noir Guide: 745 Films of the Classic Era, 1940–1959*. Jefferson, NC: McFarland, 2003.

King, Neal. *Heroes in Hard Times: Cop Action Movies in the U.S.* Philadelphia: Temple University Press, 1999.

Leitch, Thomas. *Crime Films*. Cambridge: Cambridge University Press, 2002.

Martin, Richard. *Mean Streets and Raging Bulls: The Legacy of Film Noir in Contemporary American Cinema*. Lanham, MD: Scarecrow, 1997.

Mason, Fran. *American Gangster Cinema: From Little Caesar to Pulp Fiction*. New York: Palgrave / MacMillan, 2002.

Muller, Eddie. *Dark City: The Lost World of Film Noir*. New York: St. Martin's / Griffin, 1998.

———. *Dark City Dames: The Wicked Women of Film Noir*. New York: Regan Books / Harper Collins, 2001.

Palmer, R. Burton. *Perspectives on Film Noir*. New York: G. K. Hall, 1996.

Penzler, Otto. *101 Greatest Films of Mystery and Suspense*. New York: i books, 2000.

Richardson, Carl. *Autopsy: An Element of Realism in Film Noir*. Metuchen, NJ: Scarecrow, 1992.

Schwartz, Ronald. *Noir, Now and Then: Film Noir Originals and Remakes (1944–1999)*. London: Greenwood, 2001.

Scorsese, Martin. *A Personal Journey with Martin Scorsese through American Films*. London: Miramax, 1997.

Sennett, Ted. *Murder on Tape*. New York: Billiard Books, 1997.

Silver, Alain, and Robert Porfirio, eds. *Film Noir Reader 3*. New York: Limelight, 2002.

Silver, Alain, and James Ursini, eds. *Film Noir Reader*. New York: Limelight, 1996.

———. *Film Noir Reader 2*. New York: Limelight, 1998.

———. *Film Noir Reader 4*. New York: Limelight, 2004.

Silver, Alain, James Ursini, and Paul Duncan, eds. *Film Noir*. Taschen Film Series. Cologne, Germany: Taschen, 2004.

Silver, Alain, and Elizabeth Ward, eds. *Film Noir: An Encyclopedic Reference to the American Style*, 3rd ed. Woodstock, NY: Overlook, 1992.

Spicer, Andrew. *Film Noir*. Halow, England: Longman, 1997.

Stephens, Michael. *Film Noir: A Comprehensive Illustrated Reference*. Jefferson, NC: McFarland, 1995.

————. *The Gangster Film: A Comprehensive, Illustrated Reference to People, Films and Terms*. Jefferson, NC: McFarland, 1996.

Time Out Film Guide. 12th ed. Ed. John Pym. London: Penguin, 2003.

TLA Video and DVD Movie Guide: 2002–2003. Ed. David Bleiler. New York: St. Martin's / Griffin, 2001.

Variety Movie Guide 2000. Ed. Derek Elley. New York: Perigee Books, 2000.

Videohound's Golden Movie Retriever 2003. Ed. Jim Craddock. Farmington, MN: Thompson / Gale, 2002.

Wager, Jans B. *Dangerous Dames: Women and Representation in the Weimar Street Film and Film Noir*. Athens, OH: Ohio University Press, 1997.

Note: There may be more up-to-date editions of some of the reference titles mentioned above.

Electronic Sources

Visit the following websites for information on any title mentioned in this book:

All Movies: www.allmovies.com
Internet Movie Database: www.imdb.com
New York Daily News: www.nynews.com
New York Post: www.nypost.com
New York Times: www.nytimes.com
TV Guide: www.tvguide.com
Variety: www.variety.com

Index

Page references for main entries appear in **boldface type**.

~

About the Author

Ronald Schwartz is professor of Romance languages and film at the City University of New York. He is the author of seven books on Spanish and Latin American literature and film. He has also taught graduate and undergraduate courses on film noir and neo-noir at City University, the New School for Social Research, and Columbia University. He lives on the Upper West Side of Manhattan with his wife and will eventually settle in Madison, Georgia, to ride horses and write.